Campaign to Protect
Rural England

ICONS OF ENGLAND

Think
BOOKS

First published in Great Britain by Think Books in 2008
This edition published in 2008 by Think Books, an imprint of Pan Macmillan Ltd
Pan Macmillan, 20 New Wharf Road, London N1 9RR, Basingstoke and Oxford
Associated companies throughout the world
www.panmacmillan.com
www.think-books.com

ISBN: 978-1-84525-054-6

Text ©: Pan Macmillan Ltd, CPRE, Think Publishing
Design ©: Think Publishing

Editor: Jackie Scully
Designer: Sally Laver
For Think Books: Tania Adams, Camilla Doodson, Emma Jones, Octavia Lamb and Marion Thompson.
For CPRE: Bill Bryson, Nicola Frank and Dan McLean.

1 3 5 7 9 8 6 4 2 1

A CIP catalogue record for this book is available from the British Library.

Printed in Italy by Printer Trento S.r.l

Visit www.panmacmillan.com to read more about all our books and to buy them. You will also find features,
author interviews and news of any author events, and you can sign up for e-newsletters so that you're always
first to hear about our new releases.

Cover image: Alamy

The Campaign to Protect Rural England warmly thanks all those who have contributed words and photographs to this book. We dedicate it to the many thousands of volunteers who have worked so hard and given so freely of their time since we were founded in 1926.

Campaign to Protect
Rural England

FOREWORD

Jackie Scully, Editor, *Icons of England*

The experience of reading this book is very much like visiting the New Forest. Go in search of a densely packed and rather young-looking Hampshire forest – as the name suggests – and you may come back slightly confused. For you will fall in love not with its patches of woodland but its wide-open spaces, time-weathered bushes and the fact that life stops momentarily when ponies take to the road. Try to navigate your way through its winding ornamental drives and over its cattle grids and you may never quite find what you set out to discover. No matter how many times you visit, you will always stumble across something unexpected, encouraging you to return.

The New Forest is the place I imagine when I think of the English countryside. According to the pages of this book, however, it is no icon. At first, this seemed surprising. But having read this collection of thoughtful essays, it no longer feels like a glaring omission. For me, the New Forest is beautiful not because of its history or even its varied terrain. I never left England as a child and it remains the landscape with which I am most familiar – although with its general lack of signposts, I do still seem to lose my way. Episodes in this forest punctuate my life. I saw my first deer in the fields near Bolderwood, lost my first kite to its skies, and experienced my first fork of lightning while stranded in a flooded campsite. I have grown up with its open spaces and occasional tall trees and it, in turn, has grown on me.

Personal anecdotes, childhood memories and honest opinions are what make this anthology so powerful. There was always a possibility 70 people might decide to argue over Stonehenge or debate the merits of England's cricket grounds. But, as you browse through the chapters, you will find only a smattering of the national icons and vernacular details you may have perhaps expected to emerge. In fact, no one actually wrote about Stonehenge, so it appears as an image in the introduction. Wordsworth, Constable and Du Maurier are among those who have already offered us a snapshot of their lives by celebrating England's unrivalled vistas. And through selected landscapes, sounds – and even smells – today's artists, authors and presenters are here to do the same.

When you close *Icons of England*, the countryside you imagine will look slightly different. You may be left with the image of menacing stand-alone trees, the thought of Eric Clapton playing Cowboys and Indians or the smell of bonfires in your nostrils. You may wish to reflect on your own pocket of paradise or draft a list of the areas we have been unable to include. Such is the beauty and variety of this wonderful nation that a single book – even one that has motivated such memorable prose and imagery – will only ever scratch the surface. The Campaign to Protect Rural England is working hard to keep these memories alive and ensure future generations have the opportunity to go in search of their own icons and adventures. Whether you are inspired or intrigued by the pages that follow, by buying this book, you have already joined the fight.

NEW FOREST, WILD PONIES, HAMPSHIRE

CONTENTS

INTRODUCTION

Bill Bryson   10

From Brighton pier to Silbury Hill in
Wiltshire, Bill Bryson goes in search
of the beautiful, varied and often
rather intriguing qualities that set
England apart from the rest of the world.

1 THE LURE OF THE LAND

George Alagiah The English countryside   16

Richard Mabey Marshland   18

Michael Palin Crags   20

Sir Mark Tully Moorland   22

Joe Cornish Wasdale   24

General Sir Richard Dannatt Breckland   26

Sue Clifford Limestone   28

Chris Howe Mountains   30

2 NATURAL SELECTION

Alan Titchmarsh England's flora   34

Chris Watson Dawn chorus   36

Graham Harvey Pasture   38

Jonathon Porritt Stand-alone trees   40

Clive Aslet Ancient trees   44

Raymond Blanc Orchards   46

Satish Kumar Dartmoor   48

SADDLE TOR AT DAWN, DARTMOOR, DEVON

3 STILL WATERS RUN DEEP

Tristram Hunt North Devon cliffs 52

Rosie Boycott Fossils 54

Paul Gaythorpe Saltburn Pier 56

Margaret Howell Protean shapes 58

Sean O'Brien Spurn Point 60

Marc Bedingfield Seven Sisters 62

Wendy Cope Water meadows 64

Elizabeth Jane Howard My island 66

Joan Bakewell Estuaries 67

4 EPHEMERAL BEAUTY

Richard Benson Rural sensuality 70

Sir Roy Strong Light and shade 72

Guy Edwardes Marshwood Vale 74

Gavin Pretor-Pinney Clouds 76

Tom Heap Bonfires 78

Sir Nigel Thompson Mist 80

5 A SENSE OF PLACE

Eric Clapton Newlands Corner 84

Nicholas Crane The Broads 86

Derry Robinson Firle Beacon 88

Dick Francis The Berkshire Downs 90

Jon Snow Balcombe Viaduct 92

Bryan Ferry Penshaw Monument 94

John Sergeant Great Tew 95

Benjamin Zephaniah The Malvern Hills 96

Dr Muhammad Abdul Bari Land's End 98

CONTENTS

6 THE HANDS OF TIME

Dr Richard Muir Nidderdale and history 102
Charlie Waite Wartime airfields 104
Lucy Siegle Totnes Castle 106
Lee Frost Dunstanburgh Castle 108
Derry Brabbs Hadrian's Wall 110
Michael Wood Athelney 112

7 THE LINE OF BEAUTY

Andrew Marr Lines 116
Peter Marren White horses 118
Robert Macfarlane Holloways 122
Ronald Blythe Man-made marks 124
Paul Atterbury Rural branch lines 125
Lucy Pringle Crop circles 126

8 BUILT ENVIRONMENT

Simon Jenkins English country houses 130
Tom Mackie Norfolk windmills 132
Dr Simon Thurley Spires 134
Peter Watson Tin mines 136
Daljit Nagra Corner shops 138
Maxwell Hutchinson London's sewers 139
Helen Dixon Lighthouses 140

SNAKE'S HEAD FRITILLARY, WILDFLOWER MEADOW

9 ATTENTION TO DETAIL

Sebastian Faulks Pub signs	144	
Leo Hickman Cattle grids	146	
David Lodge Stiles	150	
Andy Goldsworthy Sheepfolds	152	
Peter Ashley Postboxes	154	
Kurt Jackson Milestones	156	

10 THE LIVING LANDSCAPE

Alice Temperley Cider farms	160
Kate Adie Deer parks	162
Kevin Spacey Canal boating	164
Tony Robinson Mick Aston	166
Miles Kington The family historian	167
Charlotte Hollins Cattle	168

CPRE Support our campaign	170
Contributors	172
Picture credits and acknowledgements	176

INTRODUCTION

Bill Bryson, CPRE President

Years ago, when I was brand new to Britain and everything was still a mystery to me, I went with an English friend to Brighton for the day, and there I saw my first seaside pier. The idea of constructing a runway to nowhere was one that would never have occurred to me. I asked her what they were for.

'Well, they let you walk out and see the sea,'
she explained as if I were a little simple.
'But we can see the sea from here,' I pointed out.
'No, you don't understand. You walk out to the
end and you are over the sea. It's lovely.'
'Can you see coral reefs and shipwrecks and things?'
I asked hopefully.
'No, it's just murky water.'
'Can you see France?'
'Of course not. You just see the sea.' Her tone betrayed
perhaps just a hint of exasperation. 'You take the air.
It's very bracing.'
'And then what?'
'Then you walk back and have some whelks and
stroll along the promenade and maybe ride a donkey
on the beach – no, I don't know why; it's just something
else we do – and then you have an ice cream and get
on the train and go home.'
'And this is a fabulous day out?'
'Oh yes, it's lovely. Especially if it doesn't rain.'

I have since come to realise that she was right about everything but the whelks. (If you are reading this in another country and aren't familiar with that marine delicacy, you may get the same experience by finding an old golf ball, removing the cover and eating what remains. The only difference is that the golf ball has a little more flavour.) Indeed, after some 30 years of devoted observation I have come to appreciate that the things that make England what it is – which is to say, like nowhere else on earth – and however peculiar they may seem at first blush, are actually quite endearing and often deeply admirable. This is a book about those things.

Four qualities in particular, I think, set English icons apart and make them more memorable, more individual, vastly more noteworthy than icons elsewhere. Foremost among these is the ability – so gloriously evinced in the seaside pier – to be magnificent while having no evident purpose at all.

Consider one of my own favourite national glories, the wondrously artificial, profoundly inexplicable Silbury Hill in Wiltshire – the largest man-made mound in Europe. Built at about the same time as Stonehenge, it covers five acres and rises 130 feet above the surrounding landscape. It is positively immense, and involved an almost unimaginable commitment of labour. Yet Silbury Hill has no known purpose. It is not a burial chamber and holds no treasures. It consists of nothing but soil and rock carefully formed into a large pudding-shaped hill. All that can be said for certain is that some people at some time in the very distant past decided for purposes we cannot guess to make a large hill where previously there had been none.

There really is a kind of national instinct for putting up interesting things whether there is a need for them or not. You see it in chalk horses carved in hillsides and Scottish brochs and dry stone walls climbing up and over preposterously steep and craggy slopes. (Who cares where the sheep go when they get up there?) I have always been convinced that the starting point for Stonehenge was some guy standing on Salisbury Plain and saying: 'You know, what this place needs is some really big rocks.'

Which brings us to the second distinctive quality of English icons – their ubiquity. Let us rush to London, to modern times, so I can show you what I mean. We are at Hyde Park Corner roundabout, surrounded by a ceaseless flow of vehicles, gazing up at the enormous arched monument that stands on the parklike green island in its centre. Atop the monument is a large statue of a winged goddess on a chariot. The island is a surprisingly tranquil place, and in fact rather a lonely one, for few visitors find their way through the pedestrian tunnels that lead to it. Fewer still are aware that the arch contains a charming museum and a lift that takes you to a lookout terrace where you get one of the most splendid views in London. It is only way up here that you realise just what a large structure this is – and how startlingly outsized the statue on the roof is. It is the largest bronze sculpture in Europe. Only when you are up here does the scale of all this come into sudden focus. This is a monumental edifice indeed.

Now here is the really interesting thing about it. Ask anyone in London – any cab driver, any policeman, any citizen you care to collar – what the name of this arch is and hardly any of them can tell you. Although it is one of the most visible and driven-past monuments in London, on as prime a site as the city offers, it is utterly and enchantingly lost to consideration because it is just one of hundreds and hundreds of historic, appreciable, glorious, iconic structures that exist in London. Almost anywhere else in the world this would be a celebrated monument. Here it is backdrop.

Part of the reason its name is not better known is that it has had several in the 180 years since it was built by the great Decimus Burton. At various times it has been known as Constitution Arch, Wellington Arch, Green Park Arch and now Wellington Arch again. You won't be surprised to hear that

it is also quite useless and always has been. It was designed originally as an outer entryway to Buckingham Palace, but was such an impediment to traffic, and so completely out of scale, that it was moved to the traffic island in 1882 just to get it out of the way.

It is your good fortune in this country to have so many iconic treasures, but it is a danger too. Having so many means that they are easily forgotten and even lost – which is the third and most tragic of the qualities that set English icons apart. In the 30 years I have known England, you have lost, or all but lost, an appreciable number of iconic features – milk bottles, corner shops, village post offices, red phone boxes, seaside holidays and even some seaside piers, including the one at Brighton that so bemused and transfixed me 30 years ago.

Happily, there is a fourth and more encouraging quality to icons, as this book so sumptuously and engagingly attests: people love them. They don't just appreciate them, the way you might appreciate a good book or an expensive dinner. They love them like a child. National icons really are the things that set countries apart and yet they are almost always taken completely for granted, which means they often aren't missed until they are gone for good. So it is wonderful to see them given the warmth and reverence they deserve in the pages that follow.

It is also a timely reminder of how lucky we are to have a heroic outfit like the Campaign to Protect Rural England, to make sure that other iconic features – like Green Belts and hedgerows, long views over dreamy landscapes and a thousand things more – aren't lost as well.

Our job is to make sure that a book like this is always a celebration and not a memorial. We are immensely grateful to all the writers who have contributed. We were especially pleased to receive a thoughtful and touching contribution from the great and kindly Miles Kington shortly before his tragically early death last winter. He will be missed a great deal. As for the rest of you, we can't thank you enough for your support.

STONEHENGE,
WILTSHIRE

THE LURE
OF THE LAND

George Alagiah, Richard Mabey,
Michael Palin, Sir Mark Tully, Joe Cornish,
General Sir Richard Dannatt,
Suc Clifford, Chris Howe

A PLACE IN THE COUNTRY

George Alagiah on the English countryside

HOOKNEY TOR,
DEVON

'My parents live in the country. Would you like to come and stay with us?' I can't remember if those were the exact words but I do recall the fact that it was the first time I'd heard of 'the country'. This was 1967. I was 11 going on 12, and had just arrived in England. I had moved from one country, Ghana, to this one, so I was confused as to what my new English friend was referring. Just weeks into what would become a lifetime attachment to England, I had already learned the most important lesson for an immigrant – don't embarrass yourself and just pretend you know what the locals are talking about. I accepted the offer and, some days later, found myself on the train from Portsmouth to Sussex.

I didn't fully understand it at the time. But on that little weekend retreat from our city school I encountered the country – not as a place, but as an idea. Back in Ghana, or further back still in Sri Lanka, where I was born, the ties with the rural areas were visceral. The countryside was what defined a person; the town or city merely the place where one made a living. Over the decades, with a second or even third generation born in the heat and dust of the towns, the enduring strength of the extended family pulls one back to the source of the bloodline – to the village or hamlet where it all began.

Here it is different. Here the power of the Industrial Revolution tipped the balance in favour of England's town and cities. The smoke stacks and tenements changed the physical landscape, but they also altered the mental landscape. The 'country' had to be reinvented as an escape and a refuge from the demands of urban living. Sometimes the countryside has been reduced to a leisure activity, a package deal shorn of nature's life-affirming rhythm, and cleansed of the muck and smell that is so much a part of rural life. But the real thing is there all the same – every right of way is an invitation, every stile a step into somewhere gentle and generous.

I write this after a long weekend in the fields and folds of North Cornwall and Devon. In one day we walked along the bank of the River Ottery, courtesy of an obliging farmer, tucked into some of the best pub grub in Lydford village and ended the afternoon underneath Widgery Cross on Brat Tor. From the granite mass that is Dartmoor we watched a sinking sun's fading light settle on Cornwall, stretched out to the west like England's foot. To go from the verdant squelchy-welly track down to the Ottery's flood plain and then to the bleak and barren heights of Dartmoor is to experience, in the space of just a few hours, the infinite variety of this small island of ours.

The country is not so much another place as another state of mind. There is a trick to it, though. You have to leave the call of the BlackBerry behind. You need to stop when you feel like stopping; look when you feel like looking and talk when you feel like talking. And then you might learn, as we did from a local, that the reason hundreds of starlings in flight will twist and turn in unison is because the ones on the outside are constantly trying to get to the inside where they feel safer.

Some 40 years on from that first trip, I finally understand what going to the country is all about. And now it's my turn to offer an invitation: 'Fancy a weekend in the country?'

HIDDEN DEPTHS

Richard Mabey on marshland

At a casual glance, it seems the very negation of landscape. Nothing blocks the view to the horizon. There are no elevations, no shadows and no secret glades. The ground seems to have been scoured into a rumpled, homogeneous plain.

But marshland is more subtle than that. Think of it, for a moment, as a landscape whose contours are under the ground – as an inverted habitat, riddled with concavities. Then imagine it turned upside down. Now the prospect is alive with mounds and reticulations. Glacial hollows and human peat pits swell like prehistoric barrows. Dykes are three-dimensional fences. Peat layers appear and disappear in complex laminations.

Now turn it upright again. Think of the whole surface of the marsh as an outgrowth of this damp labyrinth. Resist the pull of the horizon and shorten your focus a little. The homogeneity vanishes. There are dark sedges; livid bog mosses and lustrous mist-green patches of reed. There are grass tussocks, scrubby tumps, flashes, pools and inscrutable ribbons of vegetation. And, closing your focus still further, you realise that this apparently bland and static view is in constant motion. Marshes – mosaics of thin verticals – are animated by the wind like no other landscape.

Now think of the birds that coast above marshlands as dowsers of this complex geometry of wetland and wind. Ducks explode into the air, manifesting patches of water that, to the watcher, are quite invisible. Marsh harriers tack across the Fens, rising and falling as if they were riding invisible currents in the air – pockets of low pressure, tiny thermals generated by the minute shifts from water to grass to reed. Once, in Suffolk, I watched a hobby riding the subtle troughs in a reedbed like a surfer. It was catching dragonflies, and as it soared up to eat them, the chitin from the chewed-off wings fell back into the reed like tinsel. The whole vocabulary of the marsh is about this intimacy of movement: rustling, gliding, quaking, shimmering.

Nothing, however, animates marshland more than the water that created it. When the rains come (the winter flood-time), water finds its way back into the shallowest dips and into every inch-deep depression, remaking the landscape it formed 10 millennia ago. And the shapes it makes seem amorphous and unbiddable. It slinks about the surface of land like a Chinese whisper, full of possibilities, taking new form as it goes – joining field-puddle with reed-pool, with streamlet, with river.

Marshlands are the stage for fast-moving dramas of the great principles that govern ecosystems: change, continuity and connectivity. Water is a great communicator and forms a conduit for reed seeds and migrating eels, between ancient habits and new beginnings. Sometimes when I walk on a marsh, efflorescences of water spread round my feet, and I have the feeling that yards, maybe miles, further on I'm squeezing water out on to some slumbering aquatic growths. Marshes may momentarily look inert and vacuous, but in reality they are agile, adaptive and inclusive. They are about living in the present and going with the flow.

COMMON REED
PHRAGMITES AUSTRALIS
SEED HEADS, SOMERSET

LIVING ON THE EDGE

Michael Palin on crags

I was born and brought up in Sheffield. In the 1950s, before the ascendancy of her near neighbour Leeds, Sheffield was the fourth largest city in England. Some half a million people were squeezed into her hills and valleys, and a pall of pollution from a succession of huge steel foundries smothered the long rows of back-to-back houses on the east side of the city.

I was unequivocally a city boy. My father worked in the heart of the steel-producing district. The shops, schools and cinemas that marked my territorial bounds were all to the east, drawing me back into the city. But there was one exception. Somewhere, not far from my home, where nature still ruled, a young boy could have great dreams. He could see, in their pristine state, the valleys and rivers that had driven the mills and the forges that had made Sheffield famous. The very word for this place was evocative of something strong and uncompromising – like Sheffielders themselves: crags.

The approach to the crags was suitably difficult, but for the most banal of reasons. They were accessed via a public footpath across a private golf course. I think my general non-specific dislike of clubs and those who join them was certainly strengthened, if not originally founded, by having to creep across the fairway with the warning shouts of the privileged ringing in my ears. Once safely across the course, a tall iron-barred gate gave way to a rocky path, which for a while clung claustrophobically to the side of a formidable stone wall. As the darkened wings in a theatre lead out on to the space and light of the stage, so this uneven, awkward little trail opened quite suddenly on to the edge of the earth and the sky.

It was as abrupt and epic a transformation from city to country as you could imagine. There were no fences, no restraints and, provided your father wasn't looking, you could shuffle, stomach churning, to the very end of the land, where sharp-cut parapets of millstone grit teased us towards the abyss. Far down below – or so it seemed to a schoolboy – tiny vehicles swished along the A57 towards Manchester. Below that, glimpsed between a line of trees and bushes, ran the tiny Rivelin, a stream now, but one that had cut this valley over millions of years. And across the river rose our sister slope – one very different from ours, not jagged and precipitous but broad and benign – dotted with sturdy farmhouses and green fields partitioned by dry stone walls.

It was a cracker of a view. To the west, the road wound its way towards Manchester, eventually disappearing as the valley narrowed and climbed towards the Pennine foothills. To the east, you might, on a rare clear day, catch sight of the dark satanic mills of the steelworks. Such a confluence of man and nature could coax the romantic out of anyone.

When I was old enough to go up to the crags by myself, I'd walk along the sandy, precipitous paths with my imagination romping ahead of me – taking me to the Wild West, the Grand Canyon or the Lost World. As I grew older, my father increasingly deferred to the quieter countryside of his native East Anglia. Here I saw the sea for the first time and churches made of flint and the spooky reed beds of the Norfolk Broads. Lovely country, but for one who had passed through that metal gate at the end of the golf course, it was pretty tame stuff. When I hear Elgar, it's not East Anglia I imagine, but the inimitable grandeur of the crags that loom over the Rivelin Valley.

DERBYSHIRE'S
EASTERN EDGES

ALONE ON THE MOORS

Sir Mark Tully on moorland

Cheshire is an underrated county, often dismissed as nothing more than a posh dormitory for the two great cities of Manchester and Liverpool. But, as a child, it was home to me and my five siblings – after my parents brought us back from India, where we were born. And I came to love it dearly.

The countryside, with its lush green fields grazed by short-horn cattle, its farmhouses and smart, manicured villages, is comforting and domesticated. Where we lived was also, like most of Cheshire, flat. So it's not surprising I was excited when we started the climb from the town of Macclesfield – once famous for its silk – up to the moors on the Cheshire/Derbyshire border for picnics.

The moors were wild, untamed and sparsely populated – the opposite of our home countryside. Instead of cows contentedly chewing grass, sheep nibbled coarse turf. Heather, a deep purple in season, covered much of the landscape, and weather-beaten grey stone walls, which seemed to have come from a different age, straggled across the hillsides. As we climbed up to the Cat and Fiddle – said to be the highest pub in England – we would often drive into a thin mist.

Wherever they are in England, moors still excite me. They have the primeval quality of mountains and the sea. In the same way, they convey a sense of the grandeur of nature, so much greater than anything we humans have created. The quality of the moors, however, which differentiates them from other places of breathtaking natural beauty, is their bleakness. It's a humbling bleakness, which often gives me a feeling of being small and insignificant.

Our moors are wild, empty places. Shakespeare's *King Lear* railed against 'filial ingratitude' on a wild heath, while Macbeth met the witches on a blasted one. It was the wildness of the Yorkshire Moors that inspired Emily Brontë to create one of the most disturbed and disturbing characters of English literature, Heathcliff. And *The Hound of the Baskervilles* – the Sherlock Holmes adventure that terrified me when I read it as a child – was set on Dartmoor.

Looking out on the moors I see a world without boundaries. Open like the sea, they seem to go on for ever. And in a small and crowded country like England I find this openness particularly precious and awe-inspiring. It reminds me of Gerard Manley Hopkins' poem 'The Grandeur of God'. For him, such grandeur was not frightening. He saw in it evidence that the 'Holy Ghost over the bent world broods with bright breast and ah! bright wings.' I and many others also find that the grandeur of God does, in Hopkins' words, 'flame out' in nature. It flames out in places where we humans have intervened least; places we have allowed to remain close to nature; places like the English moors. So long may they remain bleak, wild, empty and open.

VIEW TOWARDS WILDBOARCLOUGH AND CUMBERLAND BROOK NEAR CAT AND FIDDLE, CHESHIRE

HIGH PLACES

Joe Cornish on Wasdale

Being one who loves wilderness, I find it slightly sad that, even in this remotest of Lake District valleys, the landscape is managed, controlled and shaped by human activities and grazing animals. Yet most would agree Wasdale has the wildest character of any Cumbrian landscape. Perhaps this is because of the savage screes that fall abruptly into Wastwater, or the fact that some of England's largest mountains stand proudly at the head of the dale.

Although inevitably popularised by its role as our country's highest summit, the first time I climbed Scafell Pike – one misty summer evening – I didn't see another soul. On the descent, the sky cleared unexpectedly giving a magnificent show of light and colour – a rare gift for a photographer. The second climb I made was with my son Sam, who was 12 at the time. We reached the summit at 7.15am, a couple of hours after a summer sunrise. His first proper mountain had given him a taste for another, so we then climbed Great Gable before returning to our campsite in Wasdale.

I hope to climb many more mountains with Sam in the future, but the memory of his first means Scafell Pike will always be a special place for me.

FROM THE TRENCHES

General Sir Richard Dannatt on Breckland

To those who live in Norfolk, it is known as the 'battle area'. To many soldiers, it is remembered as a very sandy training area, characterised by collapsing trench walls. But Stanford Training Area, located to the north of Thetford is also the last surviving major piece of English Breckland.

The estate lies in the heart of the Brecks, a place characterised by heathland. This important natural habitat consists of an intimate mosaic of chalk and acid grassland situated in an area with a semi-continental climate – hotter summers, colder winters and considerably less-than-average annual rainfall. Consequently, much of the flora and fauna are unique to the area.

There is a diverse range of over 600 flowering plants: 32 species of butterfly, over 400 species of moth, and nearly 30 species of mammal (the most prolific being the rabbit). It also contains one of the most significant bat hibernaculums in the county – bats use the heathland as a hunting ground. And it has witnessed the resurgence of the stone curlew which, while not exclusively restricted to heathland, seems to thrive on the Stanford heath – there are currently 21 pairs nesting there. On exercise a few years ago, one of my soldiers – a resident of Middlesbrough – turned to me in amazement: 'Sir, it's like a game park here!'

Of course, this beautiful habitat hasn't always belonged to us. And it hasn't always been beautiful. In 1942, 40,500 hectares were requisitioned to provide a wartime training facility. After the war, the land was purchased from private investors and the then Forestry Commission. It has remained a training area ever since and now comprises a little over 8,330 hectares of freehold land.

Military ownership has protected it from degradation caused by intensive agricultural development – of the 32,000 hectares of heath in the 1930s, only 7,000 hectares remained in 1980, and two thirds of this was on the training area. In 1987, we decided to bring back some of the lost heathland and by 2000, almost 634 hectares had been recreated and regenerated from clearfell, arable and from introducing grazing. Almost three-quarters of the estate is now designated as a Site of Special Scientific Interest.

Stanford remains one of the busiest training areas in the UK with up to 100,000 soldiers training on the area in any one year. But conservation is never far from our thoughts. A more formal management approach enables us to provide training while safeguarding and enhancing the environment and the interests of our stakeholders. Already we have initiated the clearance of ponds for the great crested newts and made improvements to the nesting plots for the stone curlews. An area that can benefit both those about to deploy on operations and our nation's wildlife, is an area that will always be worth protecting.

STANFORD TRAINING AREA, NEAR THETFORD

BACK ON DRY LAND

Sue Clifford on limestone

Knee deep in a ford, fingers under the stones searching out bullheads; leaping across dry stones where a river should be flowing or standing deep in a dripping cavern singing with glistening towers – it occurs to me that I learned about happiness and freedom, beauty and the land in limestone.

My parents loved Derbyshire and whenever time allowed we were up on the moors or deep in the dales. Already I was being tutored in contrasts – exposed sycamore-embraced farms, valleys and quarries defining each other, the Dark Peak with its summer-holiday cotton grass or winter-cold edges of millstone grit; the White Peak with its patterns of dry stone walls and dew ponds. That I should spend my life championing local distinctiveness seems, in retrospect, inevitable.

Limestone is variegated. The pyramid of Thorpe Cloud guards Dovedale – the name alone entices me – and I am still impressed by Peter's Stone, a coral reef knoll as big as a church between Wardlow and Litton. It stands surrounded by cropped grass framed in a streamless cliffed valley. Three hundred and fifty million years ago, fish flew by in a warm sea that was nurturing what we know as Carboniferous limestone. This Pennine reef limestone is cemented so tight with fossils and remains that the water finds it hard to penetrate.

It is always a pleasure to bump into fossils: the so-called 'Purbeck marbles' are full of shells, and form dark pillars and carvings inside many a church. On polished walls and floors such as London's Festival Hall, you can find the confused patterns of Hopton Wood crinoidal limestone from Derbyshire. And on the beach at Holy Island in Northumberland you can pick up St Cuthbert's Beads, the little coins of crinoid stems.

Great underground systems are found in the Mendips in Somerset and in Derbyshire and Yorkshire. Here too are gorges – enormous at Cheddar and Matlock Bath, narrow but awesome at Gaping Ghyll. Perhaps they are great collapsed caverns, their ice-melt streams shrunken now to little misfits or completely gone, leaving the high, dry waterfall at Malham Cove. The higher lands are dotted with swallets, sink holes and waterfalls into netherworlds. Water plays hide and seek, reappearing as risings, springs and boilings in rivers. And in between there is a world of dissolving and dripping, stalagtites and stalagmites, calciferous creativity to be chanced upon by cavers, or worn down by the eyes of tourists.

For all the limestones, the common thread on the surface is the dry valley, but they do vary. The Mendips fold gently, the Jurassic oolites of the Cotswolds roll. In deep Pennine valleys you can walk along sections of dry river beds as in Lathkill Dale or the Manifold. The situation of villages and farms show where water is (or was) and in the White Peak of Derbyshire, thanks for water are still given at the well dressing ceremonies in the high villages.

Our buildings speak most when they tell local stories of the rock beneath. In Portland and Purbeck in Dorset, the variety of limestone beds are used in different ways – local masons and wallers have left a legacy of buildings, roofs and field walls of some substance. And across the country quarries abound. You can see where the houses and walls

come from along the 'limestone belt' from Portland to Bath, through the Cotswolds, Northamptonshire, Huntingdonshire, Rutland and Lincolnshire.

From mines at nearby Box, Bath stone helps give Bath its honey colour. Buxton, greyer, is wrought of limestone from down the road. But the demand for cement, road stone and aggregate for roads, runways, car parks, harbours and concrete means the Sandford and Dulcote Hills in the Mendips are set to halve in size, demeaning the place

and the stone. Which makes all the more poignant WH Auden's vision from 'In Praise of Limestone':

> …but when I try to imagine a faultless love
> Or the life to come, what I hear is the murmur
> Of underground streams, what I see is a
> limestone landscape.

Adapted from 'Limestone' in Sue Clifford & Angela King's book, England in Particular. *Hodder & Stoughton, 2006.*

CHEDDAR GORGE, SOMERSET

MOUNTAINS

Chris Howe

'England's mountains, such as Fairfield in Cumbria, remind us there is a wild world beyond our computer screens. They divert our eyes momentarily with their ever-changing light, cloudscapes and drifting mists. It's almost as if they control the weather.'

NATURAL SELECTION

Alan Titchmarsh, Chris Watson, Graham Harvey, Jonathon Porritt, Clive Aslet, Raymond Blanc, Satish Kumar

HEAVEN IN A WILDFLOWER

Alan Titchmarsh on England's flora

There is a day in late spring or early summer when, like Mole in *The Wind in the Willows*, I am forced out of the house by some deep-seated animal instinct. I can no longer sit at my desk attempting to weave a modest kind of magic with words. I must escape into the countryside and be a part of it.

I live in an old farmhouse surrounded by fields and woods, copses and hedgerows, meadows and hawthorn-canopied bridleways, so it takes only a few minutes before I am wading through wildflowers, listening to birdsong. I know some of the birds by name – quite a lot of them, I suppose – but I am especially familiar with the flowers. It is somehow more satisfying. Birds are busy, demanding to be noticed, capable of arousing curiosity in even the most indolent of passers-by. But flowers make no fuss, except in the exuberance of their blossom, and some of them do even that with commendable reserve. The moschatel, the symbol of Christian watchfulness, is barely three inches high with five lime green flowers that look north, south, east, west and upwards in the direction of heaven; dog's mercury – hardly a flower at all, just a modest green tassel – indicates that a particular patch of woodland has been in existence since the Middle Ages. And by the river, the bashful, nodding water avens rests with its round-shouldered blooms of burnished copper that never dare to look you in the eye.

I love their names – lady's bedstraw and red campion, Queen Anne's lace and herb Paris – each one a link with countrymen of the past, who gave them their strange-sounding names. Schooled in botanical Latin, I know them also as *Paris quadrifolia* and *Arum maculatum*. But it is the mystery bound up in their common names that soothes me now.

I'll find a spot by the hedgebank that borders a field just above our house where I can sit in the warm, sweet cocksfoot grass and look down on the pan-tiled roof. I'll see the sunlight glinting on the surface of our pond – bright as a diamond in the morning sun. Swallows will skim its surface, skilfully slaking their thirst on the wing; the distant whistle of a steam train on the Watercress Line will take me back to my childhood in the Yorkshire Dales, where Mum and I went off in search of wildflowers.

I still have those wildflowers, pressed flat in a rough album – their names added in a spidery scrawl courtesy of nine-year-old fingers and a first Platinum fountain pen. Underneath the tissue paper removed from our daily loaf of bread, they are held fast in their desiccated glory – evergreen alkanet, fox and cubs, and wood sorrel – each one a memory of a moment in the summer of 1958 when they were plucked from Middleton Woods or the banks of the River Wharfe. Once home, they'd be sandwiched between the pages of the *Ilkley Gazette* before being slipped under the rag rug that ran from the kitchen to the living room, where the family feet could press them flat within a week.

It is 50 years now since their names became as familiar to me as my own. They are a stirring reminder of a time when life was beginning to reveal its riches, its joys, its complexities and its heartbreaks. Crisp and lifeless they are now, and yet within them is captured a moment in childhood – an awakening to the wonders of nature. English wildflowers continue to captivate me more than any exotic species. They belong to my neck of the woods, my childhood, my life. Nodding in the hedgerow, blowing in the meadows and dipping their toes into the river, they enchanted a small boy to whom nature seemed more straightforward than people. In so many ways, it still is.

A FIELD OF
OXEYE DAISIES

THE DAWN CHORUS

Chris Watson on birdsong

A jumble of warbled notes tumbling down through the bare branches of a large beech tree was the starting point for me this year. It was mid January. A mistle thrush, head thrown back, was singing powerfully into the face of a cold wind from the highest point in the canopy. I was grateful to that bird. Not only did the song lift my spirits on an otherwise cold and grey day, but it also reminded me of what was to come. This single bird song, these solo notes, would develop into a chorus of bird songs, gradually stirring across the whole of England.

As the January daylight lengthened, other birds joined in. Robins began their evensong; a song thrush established a song post on a television aerial and broadcast its beautiful repertoire of repeated phrases. And from deep within the leafless twigs of our cotoneaster hedge I heard the muted tones of blackbird subsong – a quiet and peculiar rehearsal for the full performance during the weeks to come. It's in the woodlands, however, where the volume of song builds most. Agile nuthatches pipe their sweet notes from high branches and on early mornings the still woodland atmosphere vibrates with one of early spring's most exciting 'songs' – great spotted woodpeckers drumming, rattling a tattoo on a favourite tree.

These birds are our resident solo performers, advertising for a mate or establishing and defending a territory. During February we can isolate and localise these individuals as pin-points of sound in the awakening woodland canopy. And then, one day in March, when the sound builds and the intensity increases, there is a change. I hear it twice or more before I actually stop and listen... Is it the end of a wren's song? An aberrant chaffinch phrase? No. It is the sound of the first willow warbler. Unseen but clearly heard – a silvery descending song from somewhere above. Within moments my ears also pick up another recent migrant's tune – the jazz-like rhythm of the onomatopoeic chiffchaff. Over the next couple of weeks these warblers are joined by redstarts, pied flycatchers and secretive blackcaps. Eventually the line-up is complete.

In late April, I always keep a weather eye open for a high-pressure system over Northumberland, and then make my move. I arrive on the edge of 'my' woodland in the middle of the night (around 2.30am) and cable a stereo microphone 60 metres away, underneath a small stand of oak trees. Perched on my camping stool, with headphones on, I listen and wait. At 3.12am, a redstart sings and is quickly followed by a robin – with a territorial reply across the clearing – then songthrush, wren and blackbird.

The notes, phrases and songs mix and melt into a rich wall of sound and this dawn chorus seems to light the spark for sunrise. At our latitudes I believe we have the very best dawn chorus in the world. Characterised by its slow development – a kind of evolution each new year – all the solo performances coalesce into a new sound and release an outpouring of song from our woodlands. It's our own private chorus that transforms the darkness into light.

GREAT SPOTTED
WOODPECKER

PASTURES NEW

Graham Harvey on species-rich grassland

Alongside our house on Exmoor we have a small, steeply sloping pasture field known locally as 'the cliff'. The gradient is so lethal that no one has ever dared venture on to it with a tractor. And so it remains – unlike most grass fields in Britain – free from meddling hands, weed-killers and nitrate fertilisers. It's exactly the way nature intended.

In June, the field is festooned with wild flowers – rough hawkbit, clover, birdsfoot trefoil, known to the locals as bacon-and-egg, and burnet saxifrage. At times it looks more like a Constable painting than a serious place to produce food. Yet our small flock of Exmoor sheep thrives on it. And in summer the sward comes alive with grasshoppers, bees and flickering butterflies.

Now a forgotten feature of the English landscape, pastures like this were once commonplace. At every site, the precise mix of species was as distinctive as human DNA, with particular plants offering clues about the type of soil and climate. Chalk downlands might often have included rockrose, kidney vetch, scabious and wild thyme. And on the acid heathlands, fine-leaved grasslands could be found flecked with rue-leaved saxifrage and sheep's sorrel, with its tiny red flowers.

Whatever their precise composition, species-rich grasslands were the handiwork of generations of craftspeople – the shepherds and graziers who managed them. They knew exactly when to allow the animals to graze, and when to take them off again. In so doing, they created living masterpieces.

Of course, they weren't intended as artworks. In fact, their beauty is a delightful by-product of the food production process.

These were solar-powered engines of wealth creation, producing healthy foods in ways that were genuinely sustainable. They needed no fertilisers or pesticides to keep them productive. Nor were they dependent on diesel-guzzling machines. Yet year after year they turned out most of our beef and lamb; our poultry and eggs; our milk, butter and cheese.

Today, we have turned our back on nature – choosing to produce these same foods by shutting animals in sheds and feeding them expensive grain. Without limitless supplies of cheap oil we would never have embarked on such a wasteful system. Now the price of oil is soaring – and with it, the cost of industrial grains. Soon we may have no choice but to give up our dependence on fossil-fuelled food and reclaim our neglected grasslands.

Returned to their former glory, these wonderful pastures will benefit both our nation's health and the health of the planet. Scientists have discovered that animals grazing traditional, species-rich grassland – including moorland pastures, heather moorland and saltmarshes – produce meat with higher levels of vitamin E and heart-protecting omega-3 fatty acids than meat from modern grass monocultures. In addition, they have lower levels of saturated fat and higher levels of a powerful cancer-fighting compound known as CLA. And that's not all. Pasture-farming also has a part to play in the struggle against climate change. While grain growing depletes soil fertility and releases carbon, grasslands store carbon safely as organic matter even while they produce copious amounts of food.

Our predecessors knew a lot about making the countryside beautiful, sustainable and productive. And there's no reason why we – by recapturing our nation's pastures – can't do the same.

PASTURELAND,
HOD HILL, DORSET

TAKING ROOT

Jonathon Porritt on stand-alone trees

When I was at Oxford University in the early 1970s, I lived for a year outside the city in a place called Boars Hill. Being somewhat disaffected with Oxford at that time, I rarely went into the centre and managed to keep tutors and others happy from afar. As a result, I got to know the surrounding countryside extremely well, with many long walks – and even more short walks on route to the local pub!

The footpath involved in that particular excursion ran alongside a huge field – farming in Oxfordshire was being fully intensified at that time, with average field size increasing year on year. In the middle of this particular field stood a large but not particularly beautiful oak tree, apparently in good health and very hard to ignore. It's difficult to explain now, but that tree adopted me during the course of that year; and ever since I have been an absolute sucker for solitary mature trees in cultivated fields.

You would be amazed how many there are once you start looking for them. But what are they doing there? A landowner, however many years ago, must have consciously decided to leave that tree totally untouched – perhaps to provide shelter for livestock in fields that had been used for grazing before being converted to arable farming? Or just because? And every one of those farmer's heirs must have consciously decided that is the way things should stay.

It's hard to think of a more eloquent snook being cocked at the ironclad laws of economic efficiency. Every square inch that tree takes up is a square inch not devoted to profit maximisation. Every bit of goodness that tree sucks up through its roots is goodness and water lost to a particular crop. Every outing of the drill or plough or harvester will be irritatingly inconvenienced by having to deviate around its immovable presence. By that measure, the more barren and prairie-like the farmed landscape, the more powerful a statement such stand-alones seem to make.

Of course they do make a return, but in metrics that are currently dangerously devalued. Such trees (particularly oaks) are often host to all sorts of benign predators that help control pest infestations in the surrounding crop – vertical beetle-banks, if you like, sustaining an enclave of biodiversity in a mono-cultural desert. And as far as the local community is concerned, such trees provide continuity and constancy, a small but telling riposte to those who tell us that the only thing that never changes is change itself.

I only watched my Boars Hill oak through one set of seasonal shifts, but even now I can recall the observance of detail, colour, density and transparency. And that's the same rhythm – year in, year out – without surprises. I am what I am, such a tree says, so relate to me on my own terms. When I returned years later the tree was still there, and although the immediate continuity was broken, the connection continued. Whenever I see trees like these, I feel they are waiting for us to get our act together, pre-eminent *genii loci*, anticipating the day we humans finally rediscover what it is to be at one with the natural world. Possibly not in my lifetime – but I have no doubt these resolute survivors are somehow telling us that we shouldn't leave it too much longer.

STAND-ALONE
TREE IN BENDISH,
HERTFORDSHIRE

BLUEBELLS IN
MICHELDEVER
FOREST, HAMPSHIRE

42

FROM LITTLE ACORNS...

Clive Aslet on ancient trees

England would be nothing without its ancient trees. We have far more of these arboreal veterans than anywhere else in Northern Europe. Just as Trinity College, Cambridge, is supposed – by Fellows of Trinity College – to contain more Nobel Prize winners than the whole of France, so Richmond Park supports more 500-year-old trees than France and Germany combined.

With our national affection for the Major Oak in Sherwood Forest, ancient cedars of Lebanon, not to mention Newton's apple tree in Lincolnshire (the tree sprouted anew after being cut down in the 18th century), we have been better at recording them than the Mediterranean countries. It is thought there are some ancient olive trees in Greece, but they have not achieved the degree of celebrity of, say, Sherwood's oak. We name our ancient trees. They are the subject of awe and fascination. They almost seem to speak to us, revealing something about our values and the vast span of history they have witnessed.

In Scotland, the Fortingall Yew must be one of Europe's oldest living organisms – its age calculated in millennia. Dating ancient trees is not easy: they cannot be carbon dated because they are still growing, and the tree rings cannot be counted because they are hollow. The Fortingall Yew parted company with the original shape of its trunk long ago and now survives as a one-dimensional ligneous wall. The late Duke of Buccleuch, who had a passion for trees, made a pilgrimage to see it, saying: 'I never cease to marvel at the fact there is something living today that was 3,000 or more years old at the time of the first Christmas.'

Visiting a tree such as the Bowthorpe Oak in Lincolnshire, so hospitably big the hollow trunk was used as a dining room in the 18th century, makes me reach for the dictionary. Numinous is the best word I can come up with. Trees have always seemed sacred (think of the tree of Calvary, as the cross of the crucifixion is sometimes called); their redemptive quality appears all the greater in the age of climate change, symbolising the power of trees to redress the atmosphere's imbalance of CO_2.

Our blessing in this matter of ancient trees has little to do with our forestry. Woods do not necessarily allow trees to survive to a great age. Competition with other trees causes them to grow tall but thin, so eventually they fall. Britain's ancient trees are a legacy of the top person's passion for hunting. From the days of William the Conqueror, kings and aristocrats needed open country to ride over. This parkland included free-standing trees. Gouty and misshapen – with limbs lopped off – but with deep roots, these 'King Lears of the natural world,' as Thomas Pakenham puts it, have stoically endured all that has been flung at them.

The fact they have survived into the 21st century has something to do with national sentiment, but more with a fact of history. Marauding armies saw them as convenient fuel, but because Britain was at peace throughout most of the 18th century and thereafter, its trees were spared.

Once, these trees would have enjoyed a sappy youth. They have now shrunk, as we all must, into senescence. As they collapse back into the earth, they become host to all sorts of biologically interesting intruders – the decaying timber of a dead tree is home to bats and alive with unseen invertebrates. But the most biodiverse are those still clinging tenaciously to life. Ancient trees have been called Britain's equivalent of the rainforests. And many of the most spectacular are oaks, our national tree.

ANCIENT OAK TREE, SHROPSHIRE

LOVE'S LABOUR'S WON

Raymond Blanc on orchards

Being a chef, it's easy for me to think of food when I consider the landscape of this, my adopted country. But I also think of something that flourishes in the gentle, moderate climate; something that leaves its mark for generations, but is also up-to-date and always in need of renewal; something we have to tend for future generations. I think of apples and orchards.

It seems I am not alone in my love of this fruit-filled landscape. In *Julius Caesar*, Shakespeare highlights the importance of orchards when he discusses the legacy a man can leave behind. When Mark Antony tells the people of Rome the contents of Caesar's will (act III, scene II), he emphasises the orchards Caesar ordered to be planted: 'He hath left you all his walks, / His private arbours, and new-planted orchards,/ ...he hath left them you,/ And to your heirs for ever; common pleasures/ To walk abroad and recreate yourselves.' For Shakespeare, orchards were places to be admired and enjoyed – something I have tried to recreate in Great Milton.

In the grounds of Le Manoir – in the fold of hills that overlook the water meadows of the Thames Valley – we have the remains of an old orchard. It is only a small plot, and many of its wizened bramley apple trees are too old to give their best. So we have let the ground under many of the trees revert to wild flowers and plants – snowdrops first, then crocuses, followed by a fragrant carpet of bluebells. It's glorious in every season, from the first greening of the buds and the appearance of the lemony primroses to the blossom and the humming of the thriving insect population in the dried grasses of late autumn.

This wonderful scene satisfies our 'common pleasures'. But we know that, to provide something practical for future generations to enjoy, we can't just create a beautiful space. So as well as the tiny show orchard, we are now planting a 20-acre apple and pear orchard. We are also adding something completely new but not out of character for the site – a lavender-bounded Provencal orchard with apricots and figs.

The 50 varieties we plan to use are yet to be decided. But I'm certain we'll have some of the best older local varieties, especially the greatest Oxfordshire cultivar, the Blenheim orange. This large, solid, crisp green apple – with its blush of red and haunting perfume – is stunningly good either raw or cooked, but difficult to buy, even locally. The trees are magnificent in stature, which makes them unsuitable for modern systems of training. This means a mixture of systems will be used in our new orchard. Whatever we decide, we know that we will be enhancing the landscape – not just for us, but for our heirs for ever.

Apple (and pear)-growing is one of the things England does best. And the simple act of choosing an English apple – over, say, a Chinese one grown in almost unthinkably large quantities – is a vote for biodiversity, as well as the preservation of our own traditional landscape. Old pearmain, recorded in the 13th century, is probably the only one of our contemporary English apples that Shakespeare would have recognised. But he'd agree that the names of the cultivars are themselves poetic. Ashmead's kernel, brownlees russet, Ellison's orange, king of the pippins, Laxton's fortune, Lord Lambourne, Pitmaston pineapple, and Ribston pippin are just some of the delectable choices on offer to help us give something back to our region and its countryside.

ORCHARD NEAR
MUCH COWARNE,
HEREFORDSHIRE

EARTH PILGRIM

Satish Kumar on Dartmoor

My life is an unending pilgrimage – I have no destination. Touching the earth – being connected to the soil, being mindful of every step – is how I practise eco-spirituality. Walking in the wild is my meditation. Walking in nature is my prayer, my peace and my solitude. Breathing, I inhale the air, which sustains me and connects me to all life.

Dartmoor is my temple and my church – a glorious cathedral of nature – that is millions of years old. It was formed by the powers of geological time and the generosity of nature. I come here for the breath of fresh air; the smell of the wet grass; the coolness of water and the purity of rocks.

I often make my pilgrimage to Wistman's Wood, high up on the eastern moor. It's an ancient oak grove that Druids made their place of worship thousands of years ago – the name Wistman's Wood means 'Wisemen's Wood'. The trees here hold firm to the earth to show us the resilience of life at high altitude – 600 metres above sea level on the windy moors. They grow through massive slabs of granite. Local myths and legends speak of 'nature spirits' inhabiting these woods. When everything looks dry and dormant – lichen and moss thrive. Life is vibrant here. One species of lichen that lives in this wood can be found nowhere else on earth. It is exquisite, a vital link in the interconnectedness of all living things.

These woods are rare now. Once, much of the moor was covered in oak. Now there are only remnants of the ancient forest – the wood's aura of light and shade. A place of mystery, memory and meaning, I feel at one with this primeval paradise. I find these trees loving, compassionate, still, unambitious and enlightened. In eternal meditation they give pleasure to a pilgrim; shade to a deer; berries to a bird; beauty to its surroundings; health to its neighbours; branches for fire and leaves to the soil. They ask nothing in return – in total harmony with the wind and the rain. The trees are my mantra, my poem and my prayer. Through them, I learn about unconditional love and generosity.

Mistletoe – a sacred plant – grows high on the trees when everything else is dormant. It is a celestial gift, the marvel of life in the darkness of winter. There is a symbiosis between the thrush and this plant. The mistle thrush's song signals love as a biological imperative. Give the gift of kisses under mistletoe and your love will be eternal.

The Buddha would sit under a tree for hours in his renowned posture – touching the earth with the fingertips of his right hand. This symbolises reverence for the earth and recognition that everything – our body, our knowledge and wisdom – comes from and returns to the earth. Someone once asked the Buddha from whom he learned the virtue of forgiveness. The Buddha pointed towards the earth. That became his famous posture and gesture.

The oak wood below, lightning above and thunder all around are part of the great mystery of nature. All the science, philosophy and poetry of the world put together cannot explain the ultimate meaning of existence. And I am happy to live with this mystery.

STANDING STONES IN DARTMOOR, DEVON

STILL WATERS
RUN DEEP

Tristram Hunt, Rosie Boycott, Paul
Gaythorpe, Margaret Howell, Sean O'Brien,
Marc Bedingfield, Wendy Cope,
Elizabeth Jane Howard, Joan Bakewell

A REAL CLIFFHANGER

Tristram Hunt on the North Devon cliffs

Far removed from the deep England of the South Downs landscape or Chiltern Hundreds hamlets stand the high cliffs of the North Devon coastline. Very different to the louche resorts and yachting inlets of the South Devon Riviera, this craggy coastline – which stretches from Woolacombe Beach around to Minehead in Somerset – is an uncomfortable, non-conformist, dogged, bleak and utterly exhilarating part of England. Admittedly, there are few stately homes or well-tended gardens here, but there's certainly a sense of the island spirit.

Along much of this seascape meanders the excellent National Trust Neptune pathway. But this is no Peak or Lake District thoroughfare with hundreds jostling from pub to B&B along well-worn paths. The steep, narrow routes and pummelling winds tend to reserve these walks for the hardiest souls. My favourite section runs from the elongated village of Combe Martin – once a noted mining, smuggling and strawberry-growing centre – to the elegant parades of Lynton and Lynmouth, Devon's so-called 'Little Switzerland', where Shelley, Wordsworth and Samuel Taylor Coleridge all found inspiration.

Along this edge of England, the cliffs rise up hundreds of feet tall, peaking with the arching sandstone of Great Hangman at just over 1,000 feet above sea level. Standing atop here, you can look one way across the Bristol Channel, to the bogs of Exmoor another, and the western coastline another. That is, if you can see anything at all. For most of the year, the mists and rain roll along this coastline in an unforgiving procession.

It is so damp that in 1952, the inundated barrows began the terrible flow of water, which led to the deadly Lynmouth flood. So when it comes to flora and fauna, this is a sodden scene of heath moorland, gorse and then, in the steep-sided valleys or 'combes' which intercut the coastline, great beds of ferns and mosses among the small forests of oak.

But when the drizzle clears, what a sight it is! The crashing waves at Heddon's Mouth; the steep-sided cliff edges hurtling down to untouched beaches; the hillsides of bracken; and then the mysterious granite outcrop of Lundy Island shimmering in the distance. The animal life is also rich: between the sheep, the Exmoor ponies and the famous (or infamous) garden-eating Lynmouth goats, there are colonies of razorbill, guillemot and kittiwake as well as black-billed gulls. And, if one is very lucky, the sight of an adder sunning itself on the rocks, seals playing in the coastal swell and even the odd basking shark.

Above all, what the North Devon cliffs offer is a welcome sense of isolation and loneliness. Of course, man has made his mark here stretching back to the Roman hill fort at Martinhoe on through the Victorian lime kilns to the mock-Tudor Edwardian lodging houses. But, today, bar the odd RAF fly-by and spirited hiking party, the modern human footprint here is enchantingly light. For the most part, it is you and the elements, you and the unforgiving sea – timeless geological formations, rushing streams, isolated coves and a sense of wondrous insignificance. It is, as I say, a rather different England.

BIRD'S EYE VIEW OF CLIFFS NEAR PUTSBOROUGH HEAD, DEVON

MY LITTLE PIECE OF HISTORY

Rosie Boycott on fossils

Mary Anning's fossil shop lies halfway down Broad Street in Lyme Regis. If you're looking downhill towards the sea, the shop is on the right, at a point on the street where the pavement is raised above the level of the road and a shiny black railing stops you from accidentally falling on to the cars below. For most people, Lyme's claim to fame is as the location for John Fowles' *The French Lieutenant's Woman*. Walk down to the finger-shaped pier – known locally as the Cobb – and on any day of the year, there'll be someone looking out to sea, the wind blowing the hair off their face, mimicking Meryl Streep as she appeared in the closing frames of the film. But the town's most honoured individual should rightfully be Mary Anning. She didn't sign any declarations or fight any battles, but down along the cliffs, which converge on Lyme Regis, she made a discovery that changed her world – and ours.

Mary Anning's life would, however, make a rather spectacular movie. When she was a 15-month-old baby, it is reported that a lightning bolt struck her and the three older girls taking care of her. Only Mary survived. Her father was a cabinetmaker who liked to take his young daughter on trips to look at the 'curiosities' embedded in the local cliffs. He died when Mary was 11, leaving the family destitute. So Mary started selling the fossils to Victorian visitors, who liked Lyme for its bracing air and spectacular walks. In 1811, she found what looked like a four-foot alligator skull in the cliffs. With her brother's help she gently removed it from its 150-million-year-old tomb. A storm did the rest, revealing the full skeleton of the first ichthyosaurus the world had ever seen.

DURDLE DOOR, DORSET

Today, her shop is packed full of fossils from all over the world. Whenever I go there, I buy another local, polished ammonite – a thin slice of wonder that fits neatly into the pocket of my jeans. A small gold label attached to the boxes in which the fossils sit tells me they have been found on the Jurassic Coast and are 170 million years old. They cost just £2.50. And it's this that I really can't get over. For £2.50 I can buy, say, nine cigarettes or the polished remains of a cephalopod mollusc (a relative of the squid and octopus family), which lived round Lyme Regis an unimaginably long time ago. Ammonites were free-swimming creatures that used the chambers in their shells as ballast tanks to control their buoyancy. They disappeared around 60 million years ago – around the time the dinosaurs became extinct.

I like having an ammonite in my bag or in my pocket. I like giving them away to people. I take it out sometimes and just stare at its lovely spiral pattern, a pattern that has never been bettered in millions of years. Like the patterns of a sea shell, or the arrangement of leaves on a sunflower, my ammonites conform to the Fibonacci number system. This simple system $(1 + 1 = 2, 2 + 1 = 3$ and so on) results in the Golden Number, or the Golden Ratio, which caused such a deep philosophical crisis among mathematicians of the fifth century BC as they first grappled with concepts of infinity. The numbers, which order the natural world I see around me, also ordered the world in which my ammonite was alive and swimming. It is powerful evidence of the connection between all things – powerful evidence too of just how fragile and fleeting it all is.

Around 99% of all the species that ever lived are now extinct and only a very small fraction are preserved as fossils; an even smaller fraction are ever actually found. And at Mary Anning's shop, you can get all this for just £2.50.

SALTBURN PIER

Paul Gaythorpe

'The iron trestles of Saltburn Pier stride out triumphantly to meet the inhospitable waves of the North Sea. This pier is the most northerly example of its kind in Britain and shows just how well an industrial structure can survive against the elements.'

AGAINST THE ELEMENTS

Margaret Howell on protean shapes

Two photographs sit on my bookshelf. One shows the emaciated remains of Chanctonbury Ring after the 1987 storms wrecked its solid circle of beech trees. The other captures the skeletal wooden breakwaters of the east coast. Their imagery is similar – vertical, dark, abstract shapes in the landscape. Both are transformed from their original form into mysterious, beguiling objects.

An Iron Age fort dating from around the sixth century BC – ringed with a circle of beech trees planted in 1760 – Chanctonbury Ring is a landmark that figured strongly in my childhood. Living on the edge of the North Downs as children, we would stand on a fine day and search the far horizon of the South Downs for its familiar outline. Many times we would climb the long chalk path and head for a picnic under the shade of its green leaves. Ancient, strong and dependable, it came to symbolise the Downs themselves, with their rolling lines and open skies.

But when, after the great storm, I saw the same trees stripped of branches, I recognised in their starkness the evocative power I now find in the solitary shapes scattered along our East Anglian beaches. Here too, on the edge, the landscape opens out. Reedbeds and saltmarshes merge with sea and sky; natural elements work on abandoned man-made forms, and the sea throws up the unexpected. Here one finds new forms, eccentric in their isolation, yet more powerful because of it. One can see an elemental beauty: one stick emerging from a strip of water; the geometrical shape of a rusty gun emplacement; a single buoy out at sea and the stark uprights of those ravaged groynes sloping down into the waves.

Alternately submerged and exposed, the groynes themselves – once rough-cut and squared to defend the beach – have lost their cross-beams, and the surviving posts have eroded into grained pinnacles that are sensual to the touch. Knots have loosened and fallen away, leaving smooth-edged holes as pure as a sculpture. These are man-made defences moulded by the very forces they set out to challenge.

There are other evocative forms too, that speak of past times and purposes. The spiky, rusty remnants and broken concrete slabs of a pillbox left over from the war can sometimes be seen – at other times it remains hidden under the constant shift of shingle. Here, even the beach itself is continually smoothed and raked into precise, sculpted ridges by the pull of the North Sea. Like the South Downs, this area can be seen as a purely abstract landscape. Long lines and flat, uninterrupted areas of land, sea and sky, where the slightest change in light is noticeable, convey the same awesome emptiness.

I can see why I keep these photographs together, but what makes them so iconic? Is it that they speak of our common past – of a people who would shape nature, are defeated by her, but then try again? Are they emblems of time and change and the need for acceptance? Perhaps it is because they prompt memories of one's own private past? Or is it because of their sheer fascinating beauty – not a romantic, quaint or picturesque beauty, but one that is clean, striking and in every way remarkable – that they will continue to enchant me?

BREAKWATERS ON THE EAST COAST FROM MARGARET'S BOOKSHELF

THE POINT OF NO RETURN

Sean O'Brien on Spurn Point

East Yorkshire is a little-known part of England. East of Hull – a city of 300,000 – rich arable farmlands stretch to the North Sea, which is rapidly reclaiming much of the coast. It's a place of silence; somewhere history seems to have finished with. The land narrows southwards past a heavily secured gas depot and a mysterious MoD museum, and then the sea and the Humber Estuary converge, and you're heading down to Spurn Point – the boom of the sea to one side; the quiet of the mudflats to the other. You're here, wherever 'here' is.

Spurn Point is a narrow curving landspit of sand, shingle and low grassy dunes. It's an RSPB sanctuary and home to England's only full-time lifeboat crew and their families. The Humber river pilots have their dock here. Beyond the huddle of lifeboatmen's houses, a wood of hawthorns masks old gun emplacements. It feels like the end of the world – which is why, I think, as children we liked it so much. To travel there in the old red bus from Hull Central Library was like going to the draughty doorway of the world and looking through. You could see the jolt where the North Sea and the Humber met, and the old fort at Bull Island, the ships sliding in and out – and beyond it all, a vast emptiness under the grey-white weather of childhood.

You can still see these things, but Spurn Head is changing. The locals don't like it when people say that high tides breach the landspit. They prefer the phrase 'washed over', as though language itself is a defence against rising sea levels. The last time I was there – last autumn – Spurn had just been washed over. A section of shingle and sand had been shipped off elsewhere and a section of the road had been shunted 30 yards west. Visitors had to walk the last mile. Two workmen were repairing the road with flexible nets of concrete laid down like engineering Elastoplast. They knew they'd be back soon. They, too, love the place, quite aside from making a living there.

At some time, though, someone will make a decision on economic grounds that the place is beyond saving. The sea means to have Spurn, like most of East Yorkshire – which is, after all, merely the 12,000-year-old detritus left by the last Ice Age. The sea will take back Sunk Island, that chill and eerie stretch of hard-won farmland just inland from Spurn. It will revisit Hull, which was disastrously flooded in 2006. And at some time, not too far off, it will not go away again. WH Auden said that poets love scenes of disaster, and I understand what he meant – the challenge of a big set-piece; the wreck of the fleet or an army gone under the sand. But what he didn't mention was that it helps to have somewhere to stand and witness or imagine the catastrophe. When the ground is gone from under your feet, the poet's role changes from observer to elegist. Spurn Point will see me out, but others will not be so lucky. Go there if you can, before it's too late.

SPURN POINT
PENINSULA,
EAST YORKSHIRE

COASTLINES

Marc Bedingfield

'The first thing that hit me when I visited the Seven Sisters on the Sussex Downs was the sheer scale of these 150-metre sea cliffs. This much-loved feature on the south coast is best enjoyed in the summer evening light – illuminating the cliffs' stunning lines and details.'

RHYME AND REASON

Wendy Cope on water meadows

When I first moved to Winchester in 1994 and began walking in the water meadows several times a week, I felt as if I had come home to an England I had always loved. That it felt like a homecoming made no sense because I had lived in the London suburbs during my childhood and for most of my life. Perhaps what I came home to was a vision of the perfect English landscape, glimpsed in films and on rural excursions. Here, right on my doorstep, was a landscape that lived up to the vision.

The water meadows are on the southern edge of Winchester, three minutes from the street where I live and 10 minutes from the High Street. There's a path through them that runs between two waterways: a millstream known as Logie and the much wider River Itchen. On the first part of the walk, going south, there are fields and trees on the far side of each waterway, and in the distance is St Catherine's Hill. Everything as far as the eye can see belongs to Winchester College, but the path is open to the public and its dogs.

At some point in the 1980s there was a plan to run the M3 through the water meadows. The headmaster and some of his staff attended the public inquiry and made their presence felt by humming. It sounds to me like a risky strategy for schoolmasters – they would have been in trouble if their pupils had borrowed the idea in school. But, eventually, the plan was altered. Despite the best efforts of protesters, the motorway cuts through nearby Twyford Down instead.

If I listen out for it, I can hear some traffic noise on my walks, except when it is drowned by the sound from a culvert or a weir. I also hear birdsong, and, now and then, the humming wings of flying swans. And I often stop to watch the water birds – coots, moorhens, dippers and ducks – going about their business.

The poet John Keats stayed in Winchester for six weeks in 1819. In a letter to his brother he described his daily walk, which took him past the cathedral and along College Street, where – although he wasn't aware of it – he passed the house where Jane Austen had died two years earlier. Then he followed the path through the water meadows all the way to the ancient almshouse, the Hospital of St Cross, which is still there today. He told a correspondent that 'there are the most beautiful streams I ever saw, full of trout'. They are still beautiful and you can still see trout in the Itchen.

On his walk on 19 September, Keats was so struck by the beauty of the season and the 'temperate sharpness' of the air that he 'composed upon it'. The result was his 'Ode To Autumn'. It was his last great poem. Already ill, he died 17 months later, aged 25. It moves me to know that my regular walk is much the same as his, and to reflect on my good fortune in having had so many years to enjoy it.

WATER MEADOWS,
WINCHESTER

MY ISLAND

Elizabeth Jane Howard on her River Waveney sanctuary

When I was a child I longed to be shipwrecked on an island. And I thought that to become the owner of one would be the height of exciting luxury. So when, about 12 years ago, I was able to buy the only island on the River Waveney – which borders my meadow – it felt like a dream come true. It was no tropical paradise – there was a small rickety bridge for access, about an acre of willows that had been regularly coppiced for fencing, some ancient apple trees, a wilderness of reeds and brambles and the largest ash I've ever seen. But it was my paradise.

Much had to be done to turn this patch of land into a vibrant habitat. The bridge had to be rebuilt. We made a fair-sized pond, which was stocked with fish, and a canal that ran from the pond to the drain at the far end. We cleared the way for a path and made three bridges over the canal. We introduced about 30 oaks (my favourite tree), mostly English but one or two red – the water table is so high they grew at exhilarating speed. We planted wild crab and plum of various kinds, three wych hazels, a number of lilacs, buddleia and roses – Kiftsgate, Veilchenblau, Paul's Himalayan musk and Bobbie James ramped up the old apple trees. There are half a dozen camellias, some viburnum, a tree peony, and the aconites, snowdrops, primroses, bluebells, *Fritillaria meleagris* and wild daffodil are steadily increasing.

We wanted to create something that could be enjoyed all times of the year, with provision for as much wildlife as possible. There are now hedgehogs, grass snakes, rabbits, mice, camel-coloured frogs, reed warblers, thrushes, wood pigeons, sometimes a pair of owls, and a woodpecker. Some years we get butterflies attracted to the raucous mauve buddleia and a quantity of bees that love the ivy

when it flowers. Ducks and a moorhen enjoy the pond and canal – the moorhen built her nest last year in the middle of a white waterlily that has assumed giant proportions. I also have a pair of mute swans called Bernard and Dora that have nested in various parts of the island and come in the summer to eat duckweed. Sadly, although the first year Dora laid six eggs, they were stolen and the swans haven't come to nest again. I wanted the island to be a safe environment for nesting and I do hope they return.

The island is only small but it has become a magic place for me. I walk around it every day and there is always something to notice and love. People say we plant trees for others to enjoy in future. I think this is true, but the pleasure of watching them grow from saplings to fine young trees is a reward in itself. There is also a great satisfaction in introducing plants that, if they are happy, will naturalise. Cowslips seem exotic to me because I was brought up in Sussex where there weren't any, so to see them increasing every year is another plus. The arrival of the amazing and beautiful bee orchid was a thrill, but they are mysterious and freakish in their behaviour; they will turn up one year and then disappear completely – and just as I have given up hope, appear somewhere quite different. They make plain the fact that wild flowers know what suits them, and cannot be tamed into putting up with conditions that garden plants often have to endure.

Of course, I have had failures. It is too wet for white foxgloves. Primulas do well, but the swans demolish them. Moles are a menace to the roots of young trees and mice eat the corms of anemones. But as my friend Ursula Vaughan Williams said, while she refilled a saucer of milk put out for a stray cat and found three slugs drinking from it, 'There's plenty for all'. And I hope my island will continue to be that for everyone who, in future, owns or lives on it.

WHERE THE RIVER MEETS THE SEA

Joan Bakewell on estuaries

An estuary is an awesome thing, its great bulk of fresh water pressing forward remorselessly into the measureless ocean. It is a striking sight in all weathers – the Severn Estuary below Bristol with its rippling bore; the Mersey's quiet emergence into Liverpool Bay. But the one I really love is the gentle winding of the River Alde towards the North Sea at Aldeburgh.

Suffolk is a place admired for its vast skyscapes rather than its landscapes. The clouds scud and gather over reedy marshes and heathland – you can see the weather coming from far away and there's always time to run for cover. And a scattering of ancient spires indicates this was once a thriving centre of the wool trade. For me, however, a Suffolk scene wouldn't be as compelling without the meandering river, and the wild, unrelenting coastline with its fishermen's huts and encroaching tides.

Following the River Alde's twists and turns is like watching a drama unfold. Much of the Aldeburgh Music Festival takes place along its banks in a converted maltings – a complex of red brick buildings sitting low in the landscape, whose steeped roofs are scarcely visible above the lie of the land. Below it, the river winds its way towards the desolate North Sea, always battling against its swaying reedbeds. On a summer evening, as the birds swoop and call above the water, it is easy to sit back, look out at the ancient Iken Church that sits alone on the horizon, and feel part of the action.

As the Alde widens its banks, the drama continues. A scattering of pine trees shed their cones on its sandy shores. At Aldeburgh itself – a one-street town whose coloured houses line the coast – the estuary turns south past a modest yacht club and finds its way to Orford, with its pretty harbour. This is where Britten's Peter Grimes set his boats out to sea. And it is hard for me to stroll along its pebble beach without hearing the opera's interludes playing in my head.

Beyond the harbour lies a sea quite unlike the Alde's meandering waterway. There is nothing gentle about this coast. The winds and tides can lash hard and the encroaching seas threaten nearby settlements. Some have already surrendered to its waves – they say further north at Dunwich, you can hear the drowned church bells tolling beneath the sea. It is a place to see distant container ships ply the world's trade and to hear the startled sounds of a beach-goer, who has ventured bravely beyond the family windbreak to test the cold water.

Of course, the Alde's days have not always been innocent. In the last wars, for example, they chose the desolate Shingle Street for military experiments. Today, oystercatchers haunt the place and small boats of visitors with binoculars come to take a look – though there isn't much to see. Change happens, history is washed away, but the Alde – with a life of its own – continues its journey to the open sea. And it is this timelessness that I believe gives the estuary its charm.

EPHEMERAL
BEAUTY

Richard Benson, Sir Roy Strong,
Guy Edwardes, Gavin Pretor-Pinney,
Tom Heap, Sir Nigel Thompson

SENSES AND SENSIBILITY

Richard Benson on rural sensuality

One bright blue, oven-hot afternoon in the summer of 1984, my friend Johnny and I were constructing the top layers of a vast straw stack in a field on the East Yorkshire Wolds. We were 18 and working for a local farmer in our last school summer holiday. All our summers were spent in this way but for some reason I have a clear memory of this particular day, or rather of a particular moment in it.

It came as we finished unloading and tessellating a trailer-load of bales. As the straw stack was close to a windbreak of larch, damson and apple trees, we pulled some apples from the branches and sat on the straw to eat them. They were unripe, bitter-tasting bramleys, but eating them up there in the sunshine felt good. We felt one of those small stretches of serenity that always seem to come over you in the countryside when you are least expecting them. I remember that instead of insulting each other, or arguing, or talking about pop music, we just sat in happy silence for about a quarter of an hour. It's hard to explain more than that, except perhaps to say that it was as if in eating the apples we had swallowed part of the glorious afternoon.

When I think now of the 15 or so minutes we lay on top of the stack, I have a recollection of our surroundings that is disarmingly vivid. The faint wind – warm from the baking Wolds – on my face; the leafy stir of trees around the stack; the slightly sour, earthy odour of barley straw and the virile green scent of summer verges that one almost tastes. Apart from the nursery-blue sky with its infant thunder clouds, though, there is no meaningful visual element to this memory. I think this is telling, and I mention it here because I think it is easy to forget the powerful sensuality of the English countryside and the impression it can make on us.

Fortunately, you do not have to lie on top of a straw stack to experience this. It suffices to simply walk down a green lane, stop and close your eyes for a full minute. Listen, smell, feel, suck the air in, and the place enters into you in a way that it cannot when you merely stand admiring a view. Marvellous vistas are all very well, but looking at them can make you feel separate from the landscape; how often do you hear someone say that a view looks 'unreal', or that they 'cannot take it in'? In contrast, although we may be barely conscious of what our other four senses are registering, it is often via these sensations that we viscerally cognise the countryside when we are in it.

The English landscape is not especially sensual, but it does have a distinctive ease and quiet luxuriance. It is generally moist, lush and soft, with ample curves and sibilance; its weather does not punish with extremes; our wildlife is pretty, timid and unthreatening. It has its celebrated all-time-classic sensations, such as the smell of fresh hay, the cawing of rooks and the feel of sea spray, but the dearest are likely to be personal.

Those I would take to my boring, dry desert island would include the fragrance of peas harvested on a summer evening; the foot-feel of frozen mud ruts under your boots on an early January morning and the keening of an invisible light aircraft, pleasant because it points up the silence. I might also add the taste of wild fruit – chiefly in memory of that perfect moment from my childhood. Talking about it years later, Johnny and I agreed that it was probably the first time we became fully aware of the infinite, indifferent splendour of the countryside. This might seem strange, given that we had grown up there, but it isn't really. Those most familiar with a place can be the slowest to understand it – particularly, if they think too much about what it looks like.

THE LIGHT OF DAY

Sir Roy Strong on light and shade

For those who live in the country, the two most important days of the year are the winter and summer solstice. The summer one signals that the evenings will henceforth draw in – dusk falling progressively ever earlier until, by December, it can be pitch dark by five. And, a little before Christmas comes the shortest day and the winter solstice – a signal that the days will begin to lighten and lengthen.

All of this passes virtually unnoticed in the city. Country living, however, exposes you to a whole range of natural light and shade effects of a kind unknown to urban man. The shift from getting up in the dark to arising in the light is a dramatic one. The night sky continues to be uniquely experienced in all its spangled glory. And to step out in summer and turn the eyes heavenwards is the source of an unforgettable delight.

Light conditions one's whole existence. It influences the orientation of a house – its aspect and which rooms are bathed in morning or evening light. How that light changes with the seasons and falls through the window of each room is a source of much fascination. The garden also springs to mind, for it affects where things are planted and whether or not they will thrive.

Garden making is an essay in design in terms of the manipulation of natural light, taking the visitor through contrasting effects, from gloom to dappled to the full glare of the sun.

Nature has a great way of using light and shade to turn a countryside scene into a work of art. These natural tools give the landscape its depth – establishing foreground and distance – and accentuate the geometry imposed by cultivation. And, because all of this is in a perpetual state of flux from one day to the next, the masterpiece is never the same. Rivers, streams or ponds are animated by the coming and going of light – making it refract and sparkle or appear dense and mysterious. Each shaft of light catches a different detail; each dawn illuminates an otherwise hidden beauty.

For the vast majority of the population, light is and will always be something you get at the flick of a switch. It is there at the top of a lamp-post, beaming away and dispelling any difference between night and day. The stars hardly exist in the city. But here in the country I can still give thanks that light is what God intended it to be. Only in a landscape without artificial brightness does his great creative command: 'Let there be light' still hold true.

LIGHT FALLS ON A
WOODLAND TRACK

MARSHWOOD VALE

Guy Edwardes

'This patchwork of fields, hedgerows and pockets of woodland in Dorset is often partly concealed beneath a terrific dawn mist. The landscape is made up of many farms and, due to its steep terrain, has changed little in the last few decades. Long may it continue.'

WHATEVER THE WEATHER

Gavin Pretor-Pinney on clouds

Samuel Johnson was always one for observation. 'It is commonly observed,' he once wrote, 'that when two Englishmen meet, their first talk is of the weather.' This is still true today, though it is perhaps less remarkable: with the uncertainties of climate change, you can probably say the same about most nationalities.

Some claim that our love of discussing the weather stems from some social unease – that debating the chances of rain before tea merely serves to deflect attention from less anodyne matters. This is a very clichéd and outdated image of the English. The fact of the matter is that we have a lot to say about the English weather because there is a lot of it going on.

The British Isles inhabit latitudes where warm tropical air and cold polar air battle for supremacy, the North Atlantic being their favourite zone of conflict. England is one of the first in line to receive these meteorological skirmishes as they head west. But our island position, in close proximity to the warm waters of the Gulf Stream, also ensures that our winters are much milder than elsewhere at equivalent latitudes.

The unpredictability of the English weather seems, inevitably, to turn our discussions into moans: it is too damp, too cold, too cloudy... Yet the wild, changing, seasonal glory of our weather has shaped the beautiful English countryside. Why do so many of us yearn for the clear blue skies of California, Spain or Australia? They seem to represent, in our collective mind's eye, not just an idea of paradise, but nostalgia for the endless and cloudless summer days of our childhood. We dismiss clouds;

they are brutish harbingers of bad weather and bad times. This attitude has even infiltrated our language. We talk in a derogatory way about someone with their 'head in clouds', or shiver with a sense of foreboding at the prospect of a 'cloud on the horizon'. 'Blue-sky thinking', on the other hand, has more positive connotations.

This is a form of madness. Why must we continue to believe the grass is greener where the skies are relentlessly blue? The English weather has sculpted the contours of our uplands and nourished the mossy woodlands of our valleys; it is as varied as the landscape itself. There is nothing more exquisite than a soft warm day in early May when the hawthorn is heavy with blossom and the grass a lush green from winter rains. What can match the invigorating howl of an autumn gale (especially when you are tucked up warm inside)? Or the muffled crunch of footsteps on a winter morning when the world lies a foot deep in fresh snow?

The clouds of England are not just rain-filled annoyances. They bring beauty to our sunsets, nourishment to our gardens and ever-changing airy sculptures to our skies. Our clouds are ethereal, majestic works of art that are also the most egalitarian of nature's displays, available to us all. Everyone has a ringside seat and you don't have to live in an area of outstanding beauty to appreciate them.

The Victorian critic, John Ruskin, said, 'For me, nothing has ever rivalled the variety and drama of clouds.' These free displays of abstract art, so much a part of the English climate, are something to be celebrated.

ST PAUL'S WALDEN CHURCH, HERTFORDSHIRE

BONFIRE NIGHT

Tom Heap on fires

To toss a dense mass of ivy into the blazing maw is to hear the gardeners' equivalent of bursting bubble-wrap. It crackles fiercely as though the fire itself was driven to grateful, riotous applause for such fuel. The moral satisfaction of destroying the creeping strangler adds to the pleasure; marred only a moment later when hot ivy leaf cinders sting bare flesh.

But that is the sugar rush of bonfires. They also deliver more sustained nourishment to the outdoor soul. I grew up with a rambling garden of just over an acre that needed rigorous restraining. Such restraint began with the chainsaw and the axe but always ended a few weeks or months later with the bonfire. I watched my dad in the glow. I was taught respect for the magnetic danger of flames. He enjoyed the careful planning and feeding frenzy which makes a good flare up. Grandpa, though, was the kind of allotment fire starter who could set flames in an unpromising sludge of old grass and garden debris, yet keep it smouldering for days, leaving only a perfect potash.

It is difficult to avoid nostalgia with bonfires. I guess it's the smell – the sense that delivers such solid linkage to the past it can feel like time travel. The most powerful such sensation was at Glastonbury Abbey about 10 years ago. It was a still November evening with a setting sun and a light mist evolving at eye level. The mist was infused with woodsmoke from an invisible bonfire. While I'm not given to new-age mysticism – in fact, I'm usually scathing – the scent delivered an immediate sense of history. I could almost smell the past. I fully expected King Arthur and Guinevere to emerge through a ruined arch.

Bonfire night delivers a tangible link to the past but it's the contemporary impact I treasure. If I ruled Britain I'd make it a public holiday. Despite its historic divisiveness, I've found it now to be one of our most inclusive festivals. When I lived in London, black and white, young and old all took to the streets. It is the only national celebration when people leave their homes and take to the parks and fields to 'oooh' in harmony and 'aaah' in contentment. It's like a group hug for the emerging winter. Families in town and country thrill to an evening in the elements and enjoy a few hours outside.

Today I live in the country but lack sufficient space for a fire. Luckily, the local church needs their waste sent heavenward, so I still get my fix of woodsmoke, sparks and smoulder. I love it most powerfully at dusk – when the light vanishes but the fire still gives visibility. As the air chills, your back cools yet your face scorches. You wait to turn in the unburnt edges once more. You finally quit and walk home, leaving the fire behind. But the smoke stays with you, every thread of clothing carrying its aromatic signature; a reminder of the outdoors brought indoors. In these days, when every conflagration is a source of climate concern, it could be considered a guilty pleasure; but pleasure it is.

A BLAZING
WINTER BONFIRE

POETRY IN MOTION

Sir Nigel Thompson on mist

A countryside without mist is like a play without drama; a poem without emotion. Poet and author Edgar Allan Poe once said, 'Were I called on to define, very briefly, the term art, I should call it "the reproduction of what the senses perceive in nature through the veil of the mist".' I think he was right. As summer fades and the backdrop changes – swallows migrate from their telegraph wires and trees are drained of colour – it is the mist that clings to life and provides atmosphere. For it is this shroud of liquid droplets suspended in the air that turns a rolling hillside scene into a work of art.

It is not so much the science of mist that fascinates me. It is the way it transforms a landscape as it descends. Mist is like a universal corrector in the way it veils the imperfections of the middle ground. It softens sharp edges and disguises the influence of man – it puts nature on show. I remember visiting the Lake District one October and seeing the mist linger over Grasmere. The hills stood tall above this blanket of air and the water crept out from beneath. It was like watching an artist put the finishing touches to an oil painting right before my eyes.

My life is one that has been spent close to water – I used to live in a water mill in the Lambourn Valley and now enjoy the view of a chalk stream near my home in Wiltshire – so it would be hard for me to imagine a world without mist. For 12 years, I laboured over the vineyard on my land here in Stitchcombe, rising in the early autumn mornings to tend the vines and watch the grapes ripen. And it was on those mornings that I grew to love mist and all its mysteries. There is something about morning mist that is so compelling. I love watching it flow like a stream in the air; I love being enveloped in it along with thousands of dew-covered spider webs – protected from the weak shafts of light trying hard to make an impression on the scene. And I love breaking through like the spires and tall trees on the horizon and seeing it rest like a blanket of cotton wool before me.

Whether it is clinging to the contours of a hill or patching up a scene with its artistic strokes, the transient beauty of mist is something that has inspired generations of artists. With its unpredictable nature and dramatic undulations it brings romance and personality to the landscape – turning words on a page into an evocative scene. Keats' autumn was a 'season of mists and mellow fruitfulness'. For Wordsworth in 'Resolution and Independence', the mist took on a life of its own, chasing a hare in the glittering sun and running 'with her all the way, wherever she doth run'. With mist, characters from literature are lost, hidden and enveloped – but always remembered.

A countryside without mist is a countryside without art. Far from the glare of city lights and tightly packed buildings, mist will continue to spend autumn days perfecting its rural masterpiece – before the evening blanket descends to rub it all away.

MISTY MORNING
VIEW FROM HALDON
WOODS, DEVON

A SENSE OF PLACE

Eric Clapton, Nicholas Crane, Derry Robinson,
Dick Francis, Jon Snow, Bryan Ferry,
John Sergeant, Benjamin Zephaniah,
Dr Muhammad Abdul Bari

WHAT A WASTE

Eric Clapton on Newlands Corner

As a young boy growing up in the 1950s, country life was pretty much all I knew. My family lived in Ripley, Surrey, right on the edge of the village green and, as a result, my pursuits were simple, healthy and modest – mainly consisting of imaginary games of Cowboys and Indians in the nearby woods. Visits to other villages and towns were few and far between. And a trip to Guildford, which was only about six miles away, was a special event.

In the summer, however, there were often village junkets to the seaside. The British Legion or one of the pubs in the high street would usually organise these excursions, ferrying us down in ancient charabancs to places like Bognor, Brighton or Littlehampton. And they were always memorable – mainly for the humorous misfortunes of people getting lost or left behind, breakdowns miles from anywhere and incredible singsongs there, with beer-fuelled ones on the way back. I loved the way we would amble through the strange new countryside at 20 miles per hour, everyone buzzing with excitement. And I loved being caught up in the thrill of leaving the village behind, heading into the unknown.

For me, the sight of unfamiliar landscape was like a drug. I would look forward to it all through the winter, and it spawned something in me which has never died – a compulsion to travel. Several landmarks were burned into my memory back then: Bury Hill, a place so steep we usually had to get out and push the coach; Newlands Corner, which was the first sign of the mystical lands beyond the borders of Ripley; and the sight and smell of the sea as we approached the coast – coupled with the mad scramble to the front of the coach and the fight to be the first to scream 'I can see the sea'.

In hindsight, the value of these sights and sounds has grown immeasurably over the years. None more so than Newlands Corner, an area about 600 feet high, which can be seen from the Dorking Road just outside of Guildford. In my twenties, when I set up home just outside the village of Cranleigh, it marked the final, glorious five miles of my journey home. And there is nothing better than leaving the suburbs of the town to gradually climb up the winding road until you reach the top of the hill. As you come over the crest, you are treated to one of the most beautiful sights known to man – or this man anyway.

I must have looked at this gorgeous panorama thousands and thousands of times. But it still causes me to gasp and hold my breath. It's not particularly grand – the scale of the Surrey Hills is quite small – but the proportions are absolutely perfect. A patchwork of fields and woodland is laid carefully over the gently undulating North Downs in such an exquisite design that it's always a massive temptation to stop the car, get out and let the healing take place. It's also quite a shock to contemplate just how many little homesteads and farms are neatly tucked into the landscape, revealing just how well man and nature can work together. If only man could always blend in so successfully.

It's a sad thing, then, for me to consider that in my lifetime I will have watched this amazing place evolve into a massive rubbish dump. For the last decade, a mountain of waste has been quietly growing out of the landscape. The site itself has been a sandpit for as long as I can remember, but gradually it has morphed into something a little more ominous. Its purpose is to try to get rid of things that don't particularly want to go away; plastic in all its different forms – bags, bottles etc.

At present, the authorities are doing their best to make sense of it all, researching the possibility of using the methane from the waste to fuel the trucks that carry it in such vast quantities. But at the rate it's growing, it will soon be as high as the hill across the valley – my Newlands Corner. Time – and space – is running out.

Complaining is my God-given birthright. I love it, and am very good at it. It is, however, usually directed towards someone I know will sympathise with my argument, and is therefore 'safe'. In this case, I'm sure it's already too late. I have watched this problem developing over the past few years and have done absolutely nothing about it. I have complained, but only to my wife, who patiently hears me out – then makes me a cup of tea. My complaining has done nothing other than to reveal the extent of my social incompetence and irresponsibility. I am, I admit, ashamed of myself. I fear I have witnessed the passing of something my children and grandchildren will, in all probability, never see – the beauty of Newlands Corner, unspoiled, in all its glory.

NEWLANDS CORNER, SURREY

ALL A BROAD

Nicholas Crane on the Broads

Hanging above the grocery shelves in Ludham Bridge Stores is a very strange map. Fat tubers of sea protrude far inland from a coastline which bears no resemblance to modern topography. Lean over the homemade apple pies and you realise that this is a map of the 'Great Estuary', the vast, tidal waterway which evolved over 2,000 years into England's largest protected wetland: 63 shallow lakes and 122 miles of lock-free rivers, spanning two counties and collectively known as the 'Broads'. This secretive water garden is as English as chalk grassland and sooty gritstone crags, but it is facing abrupt change.

Back in the days when Boadicea and her Iceni tribe controlled the Great Estuary, this was a trading haven to rival the Thames. The Iceni capital prospered on one of the Estuary's tendrils and the region's soils were intensively farmed for grain and sheep. It must have been an extraordinary spectacle; teeming with marine life, its five-mile mouth opening on to a glittering inland sea fed by innumerable creeks and rivers.

I grew up close to the Great Estuary's tributaries. Every morning I'd cycle to school over the River Yare. I remember scrambling through the brambles in the Roman town of Venta Icenorum, long before it was cleared for visitors. At weekends we canoed the Bure or capsized the family dinghy on Hickling Broad. And where I learned to row on Whitlingham Marsh, I used to watch the towering steel hulls of sea-going freighters creeping upstream towards Norwich. Thirty miles from the sea, they looked so utterly lost.

The Great Estuary was an environmental accident waiting to happen. After the Romans went home, sea levels fell relative to the land, and the mouth of the estuary silted up. Vast bogs and marshes formed where boats once sailed. It's a bit unclear when the Broads were formed, but for around 400 years, through the Middle Ages, some 900 million cubic feet of peat was excavated from the region for domestic fuel and for industrial processes such as salt-making. A series of catastrophic inundations and rising sea levels gradually flooded the peat diggings.

Today, this wetland moves me way beyond the reckonings of an amphibious boyhood. Every time I haul the mainsail, I know that the wind will carry our boat into a place where water and land are in a state of precarious balance. This is England's most impermanent landscape, preserved by pumps and dykes, which cannot keep pace with the rising waters. Science warns that accelerated sea-level rise, the increased likelihood of North Sea surges and violent storms look set to flood many of the acres reclaimed over the last 2,000 years. Natural England has estimated that six villages and 25 square miles of Norfolk could be lost to the sea within a century. The Broads will become saline. Ecosystems will change. East Norfolk is on the frontline of climate change.

So I no longer take for granted the river's lovely windings past How Hill, or the sight of a wherry heeling by flint-knapped St Benet's. Sail quietly, and you can see kingfishers, marsh harriers and herons attending the banks in their grey tailcoats. Otters have returned, and there are stands of alder carr where owls hunt at dusk. On the Broads, there is always the unexpected: a few weeks ago, moored for the night in the lee of a spectral windmill, I went out on deck to stop the halyard slapping in the wind, only to be arrested by two other sounds. Church bells were tinkling in the starlight, while a distant bittern boomed from an unseen marsh.

ORMSBY BROAD, NORFOLK

FIRLE BEACON

Derry Robinson

'Firle Beacon rises in a graceful curve from the Ouse Valley to 217 metres above sea level. On a good day, as the dawn light shifts and intensifies, you can see the hills like morning bedcovers tumble away in folds towards the coast. It's mesmerising.'

RIDING HIGH

Dick Francis on the Berkshire Downs

The modern-day motorist can travel from Reading to Swindon down the M4 motorway in a little under 30 minutes. The modern-day transatlantic air traveller can sit in his Boeing-made aluminium tube, fresh out of Heathrow, and cover the same journey in a fifth of that time. But both of them will fail to see the full beauty of the land over which they pass.

To behold and understand the true splendour of the Berkshire Downs one needs to take the prehistoric M4 – the Ridgeway Path – described by some as the oldest road in the world. It runs, as the name suggests, along the edge of the limestone escarpment that crosses the southern British Isles from north-east to south-west. The Ridgeway itself stretches for 87 miles from Ivinghoe Beacon in the Chiltern Hills, to Overton Hill near Marlborough in Wiltshire, crossing the River Thames at Goring. And it is the section to the south and west of this crossing with which I am most familiar, having lived in the village of Blewbury, near Didcot, for more than 30 years until the middle of the 1980s.

The Berkshire Downs, or the North Wessex Downs as they are sometimes known, are part of the chalk uplands of southern England. Chalk is a sedimentary limestone rock created from the remains of millions upon millions of tiny marine animals that once lived in a tropical sea during the Cretaceous period, some 200 million years ago. The now rolling grass-covered hills of Berkshire once lay deep beneath an ocean, at a time when the European continent of today sat astride the equator.

It is important to consider the geology of the area to understand why the Downs are so important for horse racing, the greatest love of my life. Just like in the state of Kentucky in North America, the calcium-rich grasses that flourish on the limestone base produce good strong bones in the horses that eat it. The porous nature of the chalk also means that the rock acts as a reservoir of moisture during dry summers. This allows the grass to continue to grow green and lush, while that on the nearby London Clay withers and browns.

In truth, the reason I adore the Downs so much is not as a result of any love I might have for geology. It was across their smooth undulating contours that I spent the best years of my life riding horses – toning their muscles and preparing them for the racecourse. How I loved the early spring mornings, with mist patches lying on the valley floor like fluffy white blankets. How I enjoyed the sun creeping up over the eastern horizon to bring warmth to the day. The vistas were spectacular, especially when viewed from horseback, through the gap between the ears of a galloping thoroughbred.

CHALK PATH,
BERKSHIRE DOWNS

BRAVE NEW WORLD

Jon Snow on Balcombe Viaduct

My earliest and dearest horizon, it was the distant construct that defined where my world ended and the world beyond began. Yet it was no still or inanimate thing. Across it belched the steam of passing trains, together with the flickering lights of passenger traffic that promised destinations I had never seen or imagined.

For years, Balcombe Viaduct was beyond the point that either my large-wheeled perambulator or my small legs could ever reach. It was a journey of whose conquest my older brother would boast. But in my earliest memories I never got close enough for it to assume a scale much bigger than the one I enjoyed from my bedroom window.

I grew up in the headmaster's house at Ardingly College, deep in the Sussex Weald. I shared a room until I was five or six, when I was finally allowed my own space. The nursery was divided in two and a window was cut in the wall that looked out on the viaduct. In the battle over rooms, I just knew I had to have the one with the viaduct.

In the foreground of my new and ever-present view lay my father and mother's labour of love – the garden. The lawn, the rock garden and the herbaceous border gave way to the orchard and Cox's orange pippins. The scent of the *Magnolia grandiflora* wafted up from the terrace. Beyond the garden, the lake and the nine-acre playing fields, lay the bluebell woods and, finally, the viaduct. In high summer, the green of the fields was flanked by Farmer Woods' ripening corn until the weeks in which I would watch his rickety reaper-binder laying stooks.

It wasn't until I turned nine or 10 that I – with my two brothers – first walked all the way to the viaduct. Nearing it, its overwhelming scale filled us with fear. Towering a hundred feet above us, the oval openings in the brickwork of each arch were too high for us to clamber into. We counted the 37 massive arches, and wondered how they could have been built as early as 1840 – with 11 million bricks. Every now and then the shattering clatter of the train above us would stir deeper fears. When all was quiet however, we marvelled at the pinks and greys of what I now know to have been imported Dutch bricks – the creeping yellow splashes of lichen spread like liver spots.

We never saw a soul there. The viaduct was somehow our private pyramid, our seventh wonder of the world. Yet it was not its daunting vast foot span that made it so special to me, or the number of trains that crossed it each day. It was its utter permanence at the rim of my world – somehow always there, the backdrop to my playing, my tricycling, my bicycling and my growing up. Somehow, I imagined that all children had a viaduct in their world.

It's still there now, restored, vast and busy. And although I cross it often en route to see my own child studying in Brighton, I have gazed from it, but not at it, for more than a quarter of a century. In many ways, I do not need to. It is where it belongs – on the edge of my innocence, before I deserted it and found out what lay beyond.

BALCOMBE VIADUCT, WEST SUSSEX

ANOTHER TIME, ANOTHER PLACE

Bryan Ferry on Penshaw Monument

Penshaw Monument is a half-sized replica of the Temple of Hephaestus in Athens. Built in 1844 at Penshaw, close to Sunderland, it was dedicated to the first Earl of Durham. High on a hill in the middle of an otherwise flat part of the north-east coastal plain, it dominates the surrounding land; and as a young boy growing up in the nearby pit village of Washington, it made a huge impression on me.

My father was born on the side of the hill and farmed there as a young man. He took me there frequently to see the view from the top of the hill, which he thought was the best in the world; and there he told me the stories of his youth.

For me, the plain but imposing Doric columns of the monument took on heroic proportions, and seemed to represent a grandeur and sophistication of a better time and a better place. They suggested a certain mystery, something that was missing from my life in that bleak industrial environment. Even though it was essentially a folly, a building without purpose, I was lucky to have such a strong image as an iconic focus for my memories of childhood.

PENSHAW MONUMENT,
TYNE AND WEAR

PARADISE FOUND

John Sergeant on Great Tew

There are so many wonderful villages in England that to pick out one to represent all is clearly unreasonable. But for someone brought up in Great Tew in Oxfordshire, the choice is easy. It is the perfect example of a model 17th-century village estate, with its honey-coloured thatched cottages, its Norman church and splendid pub, the famous Falkland Arms. During my formative years I came to know it as only a child does, with a close knowledge of every fold of the hills, every tree and almost every bush.

In the 1950s, for a small boy interested in climbing trees, setting up camp and shooting at birds with a catapult, Great Tew was paradise. But I could not be as wild as I would have liked because my father was the vicar. In church, we – my brother, sister and I – had to stay for his sermons, while the other children were allowed to leave early. On one glorious Sunday I remember walking through the snow to find that no one else had managed to attend. The church was empty. I was convinced my father would press on regardless, but he read out a single prayer and we were released. I vividly remember that happy day, throwing snowballs and playing with our toboggan in the soft yellow light of a winter sun.

In this Cotswold village, modern life was kept at bay. All three of us went to the primary school on the village green, an easy walk

down the hill from home. There was an impressive teacher, Mrs Bury, who lived to see the 21st century, dying at the age of 100. She taught her 30 pupils in a large school room. We would sit in six rows of desks and we moved up a row at the end of each year. Only rarely did we see a television, and even the stocks on the village green were kept in working order to remind potential miscreants of how they might have been treated in the bad old days.

Our main local town was Oxford. There was a bus once a week, but our family – one of the lucky ones – owned a car and my parents would sometimes take us if, as they later admitted, we were being more of a nuisance than usual. I was only 13 when we left the Georgian vicarage – just opposite the entrance to the church – for the last time. At that age, it took me a long time to get over the fact most people did not live in such idyllic surroundings.

Great Tew has changed a lot since I was a boy. It is far more prosperous. Many of the houses, which in the past could only be rented by people who worked on the estate – for the miserly sum of £2 a year – have now been sold. Some of the new owners spend their working week in London. In many ways it has come out of its time warp. But it would still be an obvious contender for the title given to it by a magazine more than 60 years ago: the prettiest village in Britain.

MY ADVENTURE PLAYGROUND

Benjamin Zephaniah on the Malvern Hills

For an inner-city kid who grew up in the 1960s, there really was only one place to go on holiday – Butlins. In fact, if you weren't holidaying at Butlins you weren't usually going anywhere at all. As a city kid from a large family, however, the world of knobbly knees contests and redcoats was always just beyond reach. And, looking back, it seems I had a lucky escape. For when your childhood holidays involve the back of a family camper van and the Malvern Hills, you are never far from adventure.

I will always remember the first time my dad parked up and let us run free on the hills. I felt like an animal set free from a leash. For me, it wasn't that the Malvern Hills was an Area of Outstanding Natural Beauty – I certainly wouldn't have known that it was designated as one the year after I was born in 1959. At that time, I didn't really notice the varying landscapes – the forts, rolling pastures, open commons and ancient woodland. This sea of green was my massive playground. In Birmingham, playing outside meant scrabbling over bomb sites, what we called bombpecks, and digging out old brooches and photos from the rubble. But here, in this vast space, I could play on land without fences, breathe in the clear air and run wild over the hills.

Of course, in my Malvern Hills, the hills were mountains; a den made of branches, my palace in the wild. This was a place where the nine of us could live out our adventures – not all of which were without danger. A game of Hide and Seek certainly takes on a life of its own when you have miles of hillside in which to disappear. And I do remember losing my brothers on more than a few occasions. My sister also had a close encounter with what seemed like the edge of a cliff at the time, and it wasn't until we reached down to her with a tree branch, and told her not to look down, that she was lifted to safety. It sounds like something out of a cartoon now, but back then, it felt like we were risking our lives.

I am no longer that child waving excitedly from the back of our camper van. But I can still imagine the routes we took across the hills, and the places we parked. In fact, although when I went back recently it didn't feel as big or as dramatic – I felt as if I noticed the buildings of Malvern a lot more – I think it means more to me now. Having travelled to Jamaica to rediscover my roots, I realised that, for my parents, the Malverns was not just a place to let the children run wild. It was the nearest thing to a piece of home in England.

Coming from a family where my 105-year-old grandmother has never seen a city, I consider the countryside, and not the streets of Birmingham, my real home. So much so that I now live in Lincolnshire. There is beauty to be found in its flat farming land and among its wildlife – especially a rather friendly barn owl that once accompanied me down a lane. But it will never be the Malvern Hills – my little piece of Jamaica.

HIRE DITCH AND WORCESTERSHIRE BEACON, THE MALVERN HILLS, WORCESTERSHIRE

TIME TO STAND AND STARE

Dr Muhammad Abdul Bari on Land's End

When I think of chapter 31, verse 10 of the Qur'an: 'He created the heavens without any pillars … He placed mountains in the earth as pegs lest it should shake with you … He dispersed all kinds of animals … and sent down water from the sky causing beautiful plants to grow on it,' I think of the world's most breathtaking beauty. I think of the rural Bangladeshi village 50 miles north of the capital, where I grew up. I remain fascinated by the pristine paddy fields in the summer and golden glow of mustard flowers in the winter. I think of the endless blue sky and the thundering clatter of monsoon rain that captivated my childhood. And I think of the year I first came to Britain and fell in love with rural England.

My career in the Bangladesh Air Force brought me to Britain for about a year in the late 1970s to train with the RAF College Cranwell, in Lincolnshire. And when I later came back to Britain to study for a PhD in physics, I always enjoyed taking my family out of London to explore the country's rural areas. My love for the beautiful mountains and open seas took us to many coastal locations. But nothing fascinated me more than Land's End – the tip of England in the mighty Atlantic Ocean.

Situated about 10 miles from Penzance in Cornwall, Land's End is magnificent. Even with the vast ocean on three sides it still manages to make its mark – rather than engulfing it, the giant Atlantic has taken it in its lap. Its granite cliffs are fascinating but dangerous. And although you cannot see what lies beyond the horizon, on a clear day you can just about make out the Isles of Scilly – a cluster of small beautiful islands – and the Longships Lighthouse. When the summer sunshine beams down on the water and the mild wind blows inland from the ocean, there's nowhere I'd rather be.

The first time I stood up on the tip of the hill in front of this endless expanse of water, it rendered me speechless. I was struck by how the power of the ocean and the strength of the cliffs can reduce you to a mere spectator of nature – a tiny observer of the cosmos. It is a place that takes you momentarily away from the constraints of life and makes you question the futility of your existence. Even the seabirds seem more worthy in this magical environment. Visitors come here to get away from it all, but it's a place where I feel you can learn more about yourself as you stare out across the ocean. You may be small in comparison, but it is here – where daily life is surrendered to the elements – that you can really find yourself.

For many intrepid walkers keen to explore the Cornish Coastal Path, this end of our land marks the beginning of a journey – the gateway to other places of outstanding beauty. Those who take to the neighbouring cliffs will join the longest continuous footpath in Britain, covering the coast from Poole Harbour and Dorset to Somerset and the Bristol Channel – and passing wonderful locations such as Sennen Cove to the north. It is a romantic and truly delightful path of discovery.

I wish everyone – especially young Muslim people from inner cities – could experience such unrivalled beauty. It is a beauty that will, no doubt, enable them to strike their roots firmly in this soil.

LAND'S END, CORNWALL

THE HANDS OF TIME

Dr Richard Muir, Charlie Waite,
Lucy Siegle, Lee Frost,
Derry Brabbs, Michael Wood

AN ENDURING AFFAIR

Dr Richard Muir on Nidderdale and history

Why was it that lads of the 1950s – we ramblers through nettle-, bramble- and thistle-infested countrysides – were always clad in shorts? I can picture myself in shorts of brown corduroy, with a windjammer to match. I am out in the hollowed lanes, following riverside tracks where only anglers should go, or cutting across country along the branch line, where I certainly should not have been. A border collie, sometimes two of them, would also figure in the scene.

As I roamed in that Yorkshire dale I was forever aware of heaviness in the air and a tense ache inside. It was the burden of history. I could feel the past encroaching with every breath and step, and shimmering in every wall, track, farmstead or hedgerow. It seemed like the ghosts of old Nidderdale – Cistercian monks, legionaries on the move or stooped lead miners – were tugging at my shoulders or whispering in a gibberish I could not comprehend.

History did not feature in the affairs of the village school, where most time was devoted to rehearsals for the Christmas concert. One day, however, it did feature. We were told of a Dr Raistrick, who 'discovered ancient objects'. (This was Arthur Raistrick, geologist, archaeologist and the remarkable biographer of the Dales landscape, who inspired cohorts of followers and revealed his personal courage when interned as a pacifist during World War I.) Knowing nothing of academic doctorates, I imagined that Dr Raistrick – plainly a keen-eyed fellow – must spot his ancient objects when out doing the rounds of his patients in a pony and trap. I added a little colour to the analysis by imagining that, every so often, these spectacular objects would be displayed to an admiring audience in Harrogate's Royal Hall. Though my interpretation was unsound I had, in realising that countryside places and features have histories that can be studied, passed an important milestone.

My escalating infatuation with the rural landscape proved a bad preparation for a career based on studying historic landscape. Having miraculously passed my 11-plus, I found myself a yokel and bumpkin among the urbane achievers of the grammar school. Never having encountered a decimal point in the village school, I would have no truck with them thereafter (O-level maths: 25%). My bike was waiting by the village stores so I could leap from school bus to bike and then charge for the fields in a blur of pedals and flying grit. No number of detentions could divert me from village cricket to the school's teams, and I can never recall doing any homework – certainly not during daylight hours anyway.

The countryside has remained my haven, my challenge and my sweetheart. Since the coming of the mobile phone, my love of travel has become a dread. But I still get more excited at the prospect of arriving and encountering new countrysides than at any time before. There was an old pop song by the Teddy Bears proclaiming that to know him was to love him. I believe that the better one knows the countryside – its evolution, its lost communities and its history – then the more one will love it.

TAKING FLIGHT

Charlie Waite on wartime airfields

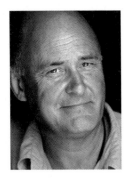

My father, Rex Waite, never told me very much about what he did in the war. Perhaps he knew that I would not take it in. He was middle-aged when I was born and so was a rather distant figure throughout my childhood, but one of whom I am immensely proud. The crowning achievement of his career was his brainchild, the Berlin Airlift – a way of getting food and fuel to Western-occupied sectors of Berlin. And an award for charity is given in his name at RAF Cranwell Training College each year – he was in the first intake in 1918. That's why, when I think of England's strengths as a nation, I think not only of its beautiful landscape, but also its people and its history – my father and the airfields of Lincolnshire.

Travelling up to Lincolnshire on a blustery January day, it was impossible not to be struck by the light – a result of the flat fields and vast sky that made the county perfect for the many airfields built here in the lead up to World War II. I found it quite hard to pin down an exact figure for the number operational in Lincolnshire throughout the war. But of those that were used, I believe only four remain. What seems obvious from this is not only how important Lincolnshire was in maintaining our defences, but also how the end of the war and the demands of modern warfare forced the county's landscape to adapt.

I was lucky enough to get fine weather on my visit. But as you drive on to the disused concrete runway at RAF Metheringham, it is not hard to imagine the thoughts of young pilots setting off on dangerous night missions to face enemy fighters and frostbite. This land was perfect for runways but attracted fog. And for a pilot, exhausted and strained to breaking point, the appalling visibility must have required a superhuman effort.

AVRO LANCASTER MK VII NX611 'JUST JANE' AT THE LINCOLNSHIRE AVIATION HERITAGE CENTRE, EAST KIRKBY

Apart from the memorial to the Dambusters at Woodhall Spa, I was surprised to find only a few reminders of the past. There are a small number of roadside plaques – names engraved on the flecked granite; there is an image of a Lancaster bomber painted on to a swinging village sign, and the walls of a pub covered entirely with photographs of smiling faces with their planes. And on a trip from airfield to airfield, it is just the odd spot of grass-fringed, fractured concrete that betrays signs of its turbulent history.

There seemed to be little left of my icon. But perhaps it is this physical lack of evidence that, in some paradoxical way, speaks volumes about Lincolnshire's recent past. The overgrown grass may disguise its scars, but the passing of some 65 years does little to drown out the voices of a thousand crews and the deep grumble of their bombers still hanging in the Lincolnshire air.

In fact, one visit to RAF Cranwell is enough to see that my icon is not just a patch of land carved out of the countryside. It is an icon of many faces. When I think of these disused airfields, I think of the young pilots who have passed, and continue to pass, through its doors. I think of the photograph of my father that hangs on the wall there – his face looking out from the 'Class of 1920'. I think of the Lancaster itself and the people – the inventors, aviators and servicemen – who have helped shape and defend this delightful country. Without such inspirational people, the countryside would be a lonely place.

IN DEFENCE OF TOTNES

Lucy Siegle on Totnes Castle

Girls, if you want to start an argument with a boy, try taking said male to Totnes Castle. 'Actually this is a motte and bailey structure,' my paramour will say, finessing my blunt usage of 'castle'. This is because he spent too much time reading *Asterix*. 'Why does it say 'castle' on the sign then?' I reply. And so it continues.

Granted it is not a castle in the Caerphilly or Caernarfon sense of the word. Those Welsh versions verge on Disney, with lots of turrets and outposts. Totnes, meanwhile, is a rather straightforward circular keep with some impressive wooden doors. Those Normans didn't mess about with architectural flourishes. Unlike Glastonbury Tor – where, in order to get the full effect, you have to use your imagination to envision the plains below flooded – Totnes has no such pretensions. It is the WYSIWYG (what-you-see-is-what-you-get) of the castle community. And it is perfectly possible to soak up its vibes without any imagination at all.

Vibes are very important in Totnes, which has more than its fair share of crystal shops; more than anybody's fair share, in fact. The castle – presumably originally constructed for bellicose reasons – these days gives positive vibes. It is accepting, gender unspecific (I normally think of castles as being male) and the perfect acoustic for playing a didgeridoo (there are many of these in Totnes).

To be quite honest, nobody really makes a fuss about the castle; and that in itself is quintessentially Totnesian. For years the youths of Totnes (a demographic that once involved me) have traipsed around the neat grass inside the circular perimeters getting up to no good. The castle, therefore, forms nothing more than a Norman-style youth club. You certainly won't find a gift shop, any loos, or statues of Mel Gibson – like those that surround the William Wallace monument.

Everything of interest in South Devon is at the top of a hill, which means we all have sturdy calves and ruddy cheeks. The castle, however, is worth the walk. These days, Totnes is a transition town – one preparing for life after oil. Meetings are held in the church across the bridge discussing the re-skilling of the local community, which must learn to do without Safeway, turn car parks back into market gardens and learn to comb and spin greasy wool into garments in the event of global collapse. Totnes even has its own currency – the Totnes pound. The way the transition movement tells it, everyone will have a part to play when the oil wells run dry. The castle will form a splendid headquarters for transitioners, although it could probably do with a roof.

TOTNES CASTLE, DEVON

DUNSTANBURGH CASTLE

Lee Frost

'Perched on an isolated outcrop of the Great Whin Sill, the haunting ruin of Dunstanburgh Castle is straight from the pages of a medieval fantasy. With Lilburn Tower silhouetted against the dawn sky like a broken tooth and the clatter of waves washing over the basalt boulders of the Rumble Churn, it's by far the most magnificent view along the Northumberland coast.'

THE FINAL FRONTIER

Derry Brabbs on Hadrian's Wall

My first encounter with Hadrian's Wall was in 1984, while doing the photography for *Wainwright on the Pennine Way* – the second of seven books I illustrated for the legendary Alfred Wainwright. I was already aware of the wall's existence but my vision of it, like so many others, was shaped solely on viewing other people's published images. I had little idea of just how awesome the three-dimensional version would be.

It was a spine-tingling and somewhat humbling experience to stand alone on one of the wall's highest vantage points, touching blocks of stone that were originally slotted into place by soldiers from the Roman Legions of York, Chester or Caerleon. The wall, which was started in AD122 upon the orders of Emperor Hadrian, cleverly utilised the island's narrowest part, extending for some 73 miles across the Tyne-Solway isthmus between Carlisle and Newcastle. Nowadays, we take so much for granted and rely on technology for even the most basic tasks. It is easy to forget just how much of our built heritage was accomplished solely through manual labour – including arguably the most important extant monument from the Roman Empire.

Sadly, prolonged stretches at either end have completely disappeared. In fact, the solid walls of many local churches, farms and manor houses reveal just how much of it was used as a free source of ready-dressed building stone. But there is still much to excite a landscape photographer. The wall can be seen at its spectacular best along the central section between Walltown Crags and Housesteads Fort, where it dips and soars for several miles over the undulations of the Whin Sill ridge. Anti-social early mornings and late nights await those anxious to capitalise on the warm tones and low-angled light of sunrise and sunset – natural attributes that are particularly essential when attempting to highlight the character, contours and definition of the wall.

I have now lost count of the times I have made the two-hour journey up to the wall in pitch blackness – spurred on by the forecast of a brilliant sunrise – only to have those expectations dashed by banks of low cloud or mist. The thought that I might have this slice of history to myself for just a few moments, however, makes it a chance worth taking. For in daylight hours, the only battles this great wall now sees are the ones generated by the increasing amount of pedestrian traffic – especially since the Hadrian's Wall Path National Trail was formally opened in 2003.

Few of those who now tramp along its more clearly defined sections will ever know that it is because of John Clayton (1792-1890) that they can still do so. Clayton is justifiably lauded as being the saviour of Hadrian's Wall. He was appalled at the way in which landowners showed scant regard for the wall's historical value by persistently plundering its stone. In the absence of any conservation or protection bodies – the concept of 'heritage' was restricted to an enlightened minority at that time – he began buying farms and other properties whenever they came up for sale. His labourers were then tasked with the job of clearing and rebuilding long sections of the wall on his newly acquired property. It is only because of this wonderfully altruistic act that this historical masterpiece is there for photographers and tourists alike to enjoy. Without him, Hadrian's Wall would be nothing more than a good story and a few shards of pottery lying buried under the earth.

HADRIAN'S WALL,
NORTHUMBERLAND

ALFRED'S ATHELNEY

Michael Wood on historic Athelney

Born in an industrial city in the cold North, it always seemed to me that the South West was the real England. Somerset in particular – the 'summer land' as it was etymologised by medieval writers – for me was the mythic landscape of our history. On childhood trips there in my dad's old blue Austin 9 I used to think that if one stared hard enough, the past was still reachable – that you might still see its ghosts. And even these days, when I go down to visit my in-laws, between the reassuring surroundings of Bath's Roman springs and the soft contours of the Quantocks, I can't stop myself musing on the tales of English history. There's one place that stands for the whole tale of this island nation. It's an unprepossessing spot, easy to miss on the A361 from Glastonbury to Taunton. But, for me, it is the most resonant landscape in our nation's history: Athelney.

The story of Athelney takes us back to the Viking Age, in the winter of 877-8. Alfred, the young king of Wessex – whom we know as the Great (he's the only person in our history to merit such a nickname) – is surprised and routed while celebrating Christmas at Chippenham. He takes refuge with a small warrior band in the Somerset marshes. The place was an inland sea in those days, a patchwork of islands and swamps, 'only reachable by punt' says Alfred's friend and biographer, the Welshman Asser. This 'Isle of Princes' was a place where the king must have hawked and hunted from boyhood, and it was there he hid while the Vikings harried Wessex. Homeless and with nothing to live on except what he and his band could forage for, his idea of England – our England – hung by a thread; his kingdom shrunk to a few square miles of watery wilderness.

'Then after Easter,' says Asser (and you can almost sense the quickening of his pulse as he writes), 'he built a fort at a place called Athelney… from where, with the thegns of Somerset, he struck out tirelessly on raids against the Vikings.' Events then led to a surprise attack on the main Viking army in Wiltshire around 9 May (under the White Horse at Westbury). Following a savage clash of arms, the surge of shield walls and the rush of spears, Alfred wins and England is saved. The rest is history.

So Athelney was the key. To find it today, stop on the A361 at Lyng Church, which still stands over a big defensive ditch of Alfred's time. At the end of the village you can walk on to the causeway, which Asser describes leading across the swamp to the island where the fort was constructed. The island is now a low mound above the River Tone. To commemorate his victory Alfred later built a little monastery here, which survived until Henry's Reformation when the last monks were pensioned off and the buildings plundered for their stone. Nothing now remains above ground.

Even swiftly told, it's an epic tale. And, of course, legends soon gathered around it. Within a couple of generations, the story was told that in the marshes that spring, the starving Alfred had shared his last meagre rations with a wandering pilgrim. That evening his men came back rejoicing in a miraculous catch of fish, and they all ate and slept well. And that night the pilgrim appeared to Alfred in a dream in his true form. He was none other than St Cuthbert, who prophesied for Alfred a kingdom of all England and for his descendants, rule over Britain (indeed, our present queen can claim Alfred among her ancestors).

The other tale of Athelney is the most famous of all legends about Alfred. The story goes that while in the marshes the desperate king sheltered incognito in a peasant's hut and was charged by the wife to watch the oven. He burnt her bread and was fiercely scolded. The Victorians loved the story, and you'll still find it in junk shops, referred to on cigarette cards and biscuit tins, and in old children's books and cartoons. (My favourite is from *Punch*, May 1941 – 'Well I suppose they are a *little* overdone,' says the king lugubriously, 'but what does that matter in wartime?')

Of course it sounds like a pure fairy tale, and scholars have dismissed it. But the story of the 'cakes' first appears in a text of the 970s or 980s, when there were people (like the Somerset man Archbishop Dunstan) who, in their youth, had talked to those who were there – 100 years is not long at all in a memorising society. I wonder then whether the scholars have been a little too stern in rejecting the story? Asser tells us that the king 'had nothing to live on'. Is it a coincidence then that two 10th-century stories about that fateful time both concern that essential of guerrilla war – food? Exaggerated it may have been in hindsight, as such things are, but it is not hard to imagine an old veteran of Athelney, sitting in retirement with his grandchildren in his orchard near Bath, 40 years on: 'Food? Did you say food? Well now here's a story. You'll never guess what happened to the king one day, when we were in Athelney...'

BURROW MUMP NEAR
ATHELNEY, SOMERSET

THE LINE
OF BEAUTY

Andrew Marr, Peter Marren,
Robert Macfarlane, Ronald Blythe,
Paul Atterbury, Lucy Pringle

DRAWING THE LINE

Andrew Marr on lines

T here are wild places. But they are not the essential England. This is an old, moist, busy, rubbed-over, scored, loved-and-plundered place whose character comes from human intervention, not in spite of it. An icon of Englishness, this Scot thinks, is the line.

There are so many lines. There's the hard-won, strong-built property line of the dykes of Yorkshire, Northumberland and Derbyshire. Everywhere, there are lines of old fields from the air, rising like undersea markings when the crops grow. Deep-driven lines of Devon bridlepaths are so gouged in the pink clay they become semi-submerged tubes of greenness in the summertime. There are the lines of copses, cut neatly round just where the tilt of the field means the combine harvester can't clutch – leaving upended pudding bowls of beech or ash across the south. There are the harvest lines themselves, parallel machine trails of darker brown on silvery gold; the energetic thrust-lines of old industrial canals, and the lines of Victorian and Edwardian railways – bold, hacked lines made by Irish labourers, many of which are now as grassed and quiet as Neolithic barrows. There are the vertical stub lines of dead industrial chimneys and the parallel lines of coal and cotton towns, hanging on to their hillsides, as meticulous and unlikely as Chinese farmers' terraces.

Above all, of course, there are the roads. From the few Roman roads, through Chesterton's Saxon drunkards' roads ('A reeling road, a rolling road that rambles round the shire'), right up to the motorways, those great earthworks driven out of London from the 1960s have redefined and redrawn England as dramatically as the stark cathedrals and castles of the Norman conquest. They have their grandeur too, and

the most complicated junctions – knotted like a sailor's demonstration – are beautiful.

For me, this endless scoring, gouging and cross-hatching is far more representative of England than any building, however fine; or mists; or even the birds and animals who are constantly moving on, and coming in, because of climate change. (My local park is all screech and apple green – the parakeets have taken over.) All round the world, landscapes are wilting, drying out and being emptied of variety by human activity. What makes England special is that here the lines are rarely signs of neglect or surrender. They are signs of husbandry, ownership, old mistakes healing and wealth taken in scores of ways without disaster.

Lines in time remind us that even the ugliest places mend. There are forests hiding the mess of the iron industry in the Sussex Weald; hauntingly dramatic mining quarries, long abandoned, in Lancashire; and the splintered, claggy remnants of Cornish tin-mining used to lure tourists. Lovely remote lakes turn out to be reservoirs, concealing drowned villages; spreading Georgian parkland hides the secret of the farms demolished to make it 'wild'. Nothing is forever and nothing is what it seems.

Thus, nothing is hopeless either. The lines are drawn, rubbed out and drawn again. No line is final. These are not lines of beauty, but lines of experience and compromise. This takes me to the final line, an echo of all that, which is simply the line of the quizzical English smile – that off-centre, knowing, half-smile you find on so many faces. The Alan Bennett, David Hockney, Beryl Bainbridge, Judi Dench smile which says, 'Been here a while, seen quite a lot, not so easy to fool, still learning.' In this land of lines, it's the line that underlines how hard the English are to really know.

FARMLAND,
NOTTINGHAMSHIRE

SCOURING THE COUNTRYSIDE

Peter Marren on white horses

s it really a horse? The famous figure carved out of the chalk on the downs at Uffington, Oxfordshire, has been known as the White Horse for a thousand years, though to my eyes it's a dead ringer for a fox. But whatever it is, the villagers liked it. Every so often they would wander up the hill and pick the outline clean so that it gleamed from afar like fresh snow melting in the sun. These ritual 'scourings' were part of a jolly day out, as Uffington's most famous local, Thomas Hughes, author of *Tom Brown's Schooldays*, recorded in verse in 1859:

> *There'll be backsword play and climmin' the powl,*
> *And a race for a pig and a cheese;*
> *And us thinks as hisns a dummel soul*
> *As dwoan't care for zich spwoarts as these.*

Scouring was a custom that dates back, some say, to the days of King Alfred, who was said to have trounced the Danes hereabouts (hence the 'backsword play'). Yet having a well-weeded White Horse on the doorstep never seemed to benefit any of the dedicated locals since, remarkably, they couldn't actually see it. In fact, even today it's hard to make out from the ground. Depending on your viewpoint, it is not so much a horse as a collection of chalky slivers or letters from some Kabbalistic alphabet.

Only from the air can you enjoy what Mary Delorme calls its 'soaring rapture'. And that is surely the point. Whoever originally cut the figure in the virgin turf of the Berkshire Downs – and the latest evidence suggests it was done around 3,000 years ago – deliberately chose a line near the top, the least visible part of a convex slope. Clearly, it was not intended for human eyes. Like those mysterious lines in the Peruvian desert, it was made for the celestial gaze of a sky god.

Perhaps that is why the creature seems to us less like a depiction of an earth-bound horse and more like a spirit of some kind, half-running, half-flying across the down. Celtic art drew from nature without being tied to a literal rendition of form and I imagine sky gods might have appreciated a bit of human imagination. And so some prehistoric genius produced something wholly startling; not so much an animal as a lithe spirit of grace and freedom; not so much an assertion as a gift.

Move on 2,700 years and we find another collection of white shapes on the downs of my home county, Wiltshire. No ambivalence this time: these are real horses with prancing legs, clodhopping feet and pricked ears. Nor are they half-hidden from view, but carved where they can be seen for miles. The best of them, in Pewsey Vale, was designed by journeyman painter Jack Thorn. He was paid 20 golden sovereigns for his trouble, but pocketed the sovereigns and absconded. (Later on, we learn, Jack Thorn was hanged for 'a variety of crimes'.) The next best, at Westbury, stands stock still as if made of concrete; which, in fact, it is – concrete having been poured over the chalk to deter weeds. And the small one at Preshute is a joke. It was cut by Marlborough schoolboys in 1805 and has what some say is an extra leg – although I can't say that's what it looks like.

Unlike the Uffington animal, these naively rendered horses, hacked out of the chalk at the whim of the local farmer, are exactly what you'd expect – mere cut-outs. Yet, when three were allowed to disappear (and a fourth ploughed up), we missed them. Perhaps we sense in them the freedom and joy of galloping on the wild open downs with the wind in our hair. They are happy horses, forever prancing with the skylarks and bees. Perhaps they embody a wish that life itself could be like that.

WHITE HORSE,
UFFINGTON,
OXFORDSHIRE

ANGEL OF THE NORTH,
GATESHEAD

THE ROAD TAKEN

Robert Macfarlane on holloways

The word 'holloway' comes from the Anglo-Saxon 'hola weg', meaning a harrowed path, a sunken road. It is a route that centuries of use has eroded down into the bedrock – so much so that it is recessed beneath the level of the surrounding landscape. Most will have started out as drove roads, paths to market; some, like those near Bury St Edmunds, as pilgrim paths.

These sunken roads are landmarks that speak of habit rather than suddenness. Trodden by innumerable feet, cut by innumerable wheels, they are the records of journeys to market, to worship, to sea. Like creases in the hand or the wear on the stone sill of a doorstep or stair, they are the consequence of tradition, repeated action. Like old trees – the details of whose spiralling and kinked branches indicate the wind-history of a region, and whose growth rings record each year's richness or poverty of sun – they archive the past customs of a place. Their age humbles without crushing.

The oldest holloways date back to the early Iron Age. None is younger than 300 years old. Over the course of centuries, the passage of cartwheels, hooves and feet wore away at the floor of these roads, grooving ruts into the exposed stone. As the roads deepened, they became natural waterways. Rain drains into and down them; storms turn them into temporary rivers, sluicing away the loose rock debris and cutting the road still further below the meadows and the fields.

Holloways do not exist on the unyielding igneous regions of Britain, where the roads and paths stay high, riding the hard surface of the ground. But in the soft-stone counties of Southern England – in the chalk of Kent, Wiltshire and East Anglia; in the yellow sandstone of Dorset and Somerset; in the greensand of Surrey and in the malmstone of Hampshire and Sussex – many are to be found, some of them 20-feet deep; more ravine than road. In different regions they go by different names – bostels, grundles, shutes – but are all holloways.

Of course, few are in use now. They are too narrow and too slow to suit modern travel. But they are also too deep to be filled in and farmed over. So it is, that set about by some of the most intensively farmed countryside in the world, the holloways have come to constitute a sunken labyrinth of wildness in the heart of arable England. Most have thrown up their own defences, becoming so densely grown over by nettles and briars that they are unwalkable, and have gone unexplored for decades. On their steep damp sides ferns and trailing plants flourish: bright bursts of cranesbill, or hart's-tongue, spilling out of and over the exposed network of tree roots that support the walls.

I think of these holloways as being familial with cliffs and slopes and edges throughout Britain and Ireland – with the Cliffs of Moher in County Clare, or the inland prow of Sron Ulladale on the Isle of Harris, or the sides of Cheddar Gorge or Bristol Gorge, where peregrines nest. Conventional plan-view maps are poor at registering and representing land that exists on the vertical plane. Cliffs, riverbanks, holloways: these aspects of the land go unnoticed in most cartographies, for the axis upon which they exist is all but invisible to the conventional mapping eye. Unseen by maps, untenanted by humans, undeveloped because of their steepness, these vertical worlds add thousands of square miles to the area of our country – and many of them are its wildest miles.

HOLLOWAY,
NOTTINGHAMSHIRE

FIRST IMPRESSIONS

Ronald Blythe on man-made marks

Following a sheep track up a mountain to a height where one would not have expected anyone to live, I found myself a few yards above an abandoned chapel. Part of the roof had gone and I was like that much-sung-to deity, looking down, looking in. Its interior was sopping wet and sheep huddled in a corner. But I thought little of its shape or state of decay. I remember imagining the person that had chosen to leave a mark on this remote mountainside. A mark that years or perhaps centuries later I had rediscovered.

I write, of course, of those marks – poetic, domestic or disgraceful – which most of us have left on the landscape one way or another during that itinerate progress we call life. And it doesn't take much to find one. As a boy I used to cut across the fields to my grandmother's cottage by way of the Gull – a deep rift below the corn. This spot usually contained the ashes of an overnight camp, crushed plants, some unspeakable rags and wheel-ruts. I never saw the visitors. But when I walk the two miles to the village now I can just hear future archaeologists celebrating as they dig up the past and turn litter into museum pieces.

Being a walking, not a driving man, I can hardly miss life's wonderful imperfections. Take the most eloquent of them, the deserted habitation, whether that of a community or a single family. The latter were everywhere in East Anglia at one point. Countless old dwellings were destroyed under Slum Clearance,

yet they never quite disappeared. All these years later it is still impossible for me not to 'see' them. A couple of miles below my own once-threatened property, there is the enigmatic Bowdens' farmhouse – now just a wired-in piece of concrete, which has a wonderful story to tell. But how can it, being wire and concrete? A poor young man who worked here was sent to Botany Bay for joining a union. And just before the Great War, a rich American took the farmhouse down, beam by numbered beam, and reassembled it in New England. It is history, of course, that lets me see this particular mark on the landscape.

My parents were always horrified – and I delighted – at the sight of a forsaken well. I would cherish the moment when I would push aside its crumbling cover, drop a stone into the darkness and count until it hit the water. If it took ages I would experience a pleasant terror. The old wells were brick-lined and stood in thicket-like gardens from which we stole flowers and fruit. Although the cottages have long gone, history has made its indelible mark.

Whenever one travels in the countryside, the mark of a hand or a foot – made only yesterday or aeons past – will always catch the eye. A year or two ago, we were driving through the Stone Age settlement by the Stour when the tyre suddenly burst. A flint axe that had been biding its time punctured it. Human beings will leave things about; they will insist on leaving tracks. And as long as they do, we will continue to be excited by them.

RURAL RIDES

Paul Atterbury on rural branch lines

The Victorians did many good things for us – not least the building of a nationwide and fully integrated railway network. Of course, we have already undone their great work by removing much of the rural branch line experience – there is nothing better than getting off a modern main-line train at a busy station and crossing to a distant platform to board a little, usually one-car, train. I still thank our ancestors every time I find, in a quiet corner of England, that there remains a way to journey into the past and do just that.

By 1900, about 20,000 miles of railway linked practically every town and many villages all over Britain. This meant the possibilities of travel, and the pursuit of the freedoms that represented, had become accessible to people living in the most remote corners of the land. Of this dense network of lines – main lines, secondary and rural routes and branch lines – the branch lines were the most important in social terms. And there were hundreds of them all over the country, winding their way through hills and dales, mostly for a few miles but sometimes much further. They carried people to school and to work, on shopping trips, family outings and on holiday. They facilitated courting and greatly improved the national gene pool. They carried agricultural goods, materials for industry and things for the village shops. And in so doing, they – and their employees – were the heart of the communities they served.

The branch-line legacy, and the society it looked after so well, lived on into the 20th century and through two world wars.

It wasn't until the 1950s that things began to change, when people and goods started to travel more by road. Left to their own devices, the railways could have responded to the challenge. The trouble was, they were not, and the old Victorian structures, which took into account social needs and benefits, and allowed the profitable main lines to subsidise the branch lines, were casually abandoned. Cost-cutting and modern efficiencies meant the rural routes and the branch lines had to go. So throughout the 1960s the axes swung and thousands of miles of railway disappeared.

For those prepared to use a map, a timetable and throw caution to the wind, the rural branch line experience is still there for the asking. By this I do not mean the preserved tourist railways. These offer a vision of railway life, but it is far better to make use of and enjoy the scattering of branch lines that somehow escaped the ravages of the 1960s and linger on in parts of Britain – still doing what they were built for in the first place.

The survivors include real branch lines, and others created by the truncation of former through routes. Cornwall has classic examples of the former, from Liskeard to Looe and from St Erth to St Ives, while East Anglia boasts an excellent couple of the latter variety, Marks Tey to Sudbury and Norwich to Sheringham. Oxfordshire has two good ones to Henley and Marlow, while elsewhere in the Midlands, the North and Wales there are exciting long branches to Matlock, Whitby and through Snowdonia to Blaenau Ffestiniog. Classic branch lines do not survive in Scotland. There is no better way to travel and see the spectacular British landscape pass by the window.

TALES OF THE UNEXPECTED

Lucy Pringle on crop circles

I am simply fascinated by the unexplained. And you can't get much more unexplained than the crop circle. These geometrically perfect depressions in the crop are some of the most striking features you will ever see in the countryside. They arrive mainly at night, defy scientific reasoning and continue to exceed expectations with their complex shapes and exact proportions. Eyewitness reports from over 50 countries will tell you it's a worldwide phenomenon. But when you've flown over the hills and fields of England, as I have, you know there's one country that takes centre stage.

I have dedicated much of my life to these wonderful formations. Following a tennis injury in 1990 I remember visiting a simple circle at Morested in Hampshire and feeling the pain in my shoulder disappear. While it is difficult to say what happened, I remain to this day an avid supporter and scientific researcher. But then, who could fail to be impressed by the sight of over 150 separate circles and 87,000 square feet of intricately fallen crop – as in the case of Alton Barnes near Marlborough last year – being flattened overnight without any warning?

Of course, the mysterious arrival of these intricate shapes on our landscape is nothing new. There are reports going back to AD800, and a famous woodcut depicting the 'Mowing Devil' – dated 1678 – that tells the story of a Hertfordshire farmer and his field of oats. When his oats were ready for reaping, he approached a mower who charged such an exorbitant price for his services that the farmer was heard to say he 'would rather the Devil took his oats'. We are told that during the night strange sounds and lights were witnessed,

and the following morning, the farmer found part of the crop lying in round circles. He was so frightened, he took to his heels and fled.

Today, I'm not sure you'll see farmers fleeing their land at the sight of a crop circle – in fact, many escape notice as farmers are often reluctant to report them. But, since records began in the late 1970s, up to 6,000 have been noted. I love the excitement that comes with viewing and examining a new formation. I love meeting people of many different nationalities who visit the circles. And I love finding out about the story behind the circles – patterns that have become increasingly elaborate over the last decade. If you played in one as a child in the 1930s, it would have most likely been a circle. But now, we find Celtic and astrological shapes, medical references and even university-level mathematical calculations. It is a phenomenon that has covered every aspect of scholarship and learning.

As yet, no one has got to the bottom of this intriguingly artistic phenomenon. Could it be they are all man-made – by mathematical professors perhaps? Could it be the result of hovering helicopters, whirling dervishes or rutting hedgehogs? I don't believe so. Or is there something more profound and truly astonishing at work? There is increasing scientific evidence of a huge electrical discharge at the sites but I believe these enigmatic formations show that not everything can be explained within the existing tried-and-tested laws and parameters of science. As Einstein so aptly puts it, 'There comes a time when the mind touches a higher plane of knowledge but can never prove how it got there.'

CROP CIRCLE,
MARTINSELL HILL,
WILTSHIRE

BUILT ENVIRONMENT

Simon Jenkins, Tom Mackie, Dr Simon Thurley,
Peter Watson, Daljit Nagra,
Maxwell Hutchinson, Helen Dixon

TO THE MANOR BORN

Simon Jenkins on English country houses

A few years ago, I travelled around England with one purpose: to write about its country houses. England has a greater number of houses with their contents intact and on public display than any other country in the world. Designed by a roll-call of eminent architects – Inigo Jones, Nicholas Hawksmoor, Christopher Wren – they reflect the aesthetic styles of their time, from the peles, keeps and heraldic halls of medieval England, to the eaves and cupolas of the Jacobean tradition and the splendour of the classical revival.

I walked Vanbrugh's Long Library at Blenheim Palace, the marble pavements of Castle Howard and the exquisite cube rooms of Wilton. I looked out over Beaulieu's river through windows cusped with tracery, examined the murals and scrollwork of Knole's great staircase and explored the green damask dressing rooms of Holkham Hall.

It also led me to houses that are less grand. East to Charles Dickens's so-called *Bleak House* in Kent, where the sea winds blow and gulls occasionally fall down the chimneys by mistake; south to Thomas Hardy's villa in Dorchester, where his second wife typed out his love poems to her predecessor; and north to the slopes of Skiddaw, where in the bee garden of Mirehouse Manor, Tennyson found refuge after the death of a friend.

I paid no less attention to the grounds of country houses; peaceful places with their graceful lawns, pollarded lime walks and meadows of wild flowers. The gardens of Levens Hall in Cumbria are sculpted with yew and box topiary, while those at Mapperton House in Dorset billow down the hillside, intersected by arbours and Ham stone walls.

All English houses, grand or otherwise, are in essence homes – refuges from the world, where people loved, lived and died. They are places of solace as well as of function; a conversation between utility and beauty. The Englishman sees the whole of life embodied in his house. Here he finds his happiness and his real spiritual comfort, as observed by the German architect Hermann Muthesius.

Today, while many English country houses allow us an insight into the artistry of previous eras, so their utility also prevails. Tregothnan Estate in Cornwall is an official safe site for the protection of endangered trees from all over the world, while Waddesdon Manor in Buckinghamshire contains one of England's finest composite collections of art and antiques, and Chatsworth has one of the largest private libraries. At Christ's College, Cambridge, I found the perfect embodiment of utility and beauty: a mulberry tree, planted at the time of James I to help the English silk trade, still in flower.

Old houses offer us communion with the roots of England, a collective narrative of its history. But they must continue to breathe, and not be preserved as museums or mausoleums. William Morris, who cherished Kelmscott Manor in Oxfordshire with a passion, believed that we are only the trustees for those that come after us. As such, we must ensure that we never allow the spirit of English country houses to suffocate under dustsheets or die in the gloom of a shuttered room. They are exquisite tributes to their time, our portals to the past.

KENTWELL HALL,
SUFFOLK

NORFOLK WINDMILLS

Tom Mackie

'Windmills and windpumps
have played an integral
part in English heritage
over the centuries. Here in
Norfolk, windpumps help to
keep the marshes drained of
water and stand as sentinels
over them, providing
an ideal focal point for
photographers like myself.
They are, for me, a true
symbol of Norfolk.'

THIS LAND OF DREAMING SPIRES

Dr Simon Thurley on spires

Boarding a train at London's King's Cross station and pounding up the East Coast Main Line, through York and Newcastle towards Edinburgh, is one of the great railway journeys of the world. Before your eyes – and from the comfort of your seat – passes some of our nation's greatest heritage. The cathedrals of Peterborough, York and Durham would make the line magical in themselves, but these are just three high points on a journey filled with historical delight and fascination.

I don't imagine many people notice the tall stone spire that lies eastwards across a water meadow just before the train races through Huntingdon. It belongs to St Mary's Church, Godmanchester, the parish church of the small town where I spent the first 18 years of my life. How could the builders of that noble spire have guessed that half a millennium after it was completed, one of the town's sons would glimpse their work travelling at the unimaginable speed of 125 miles per hour? How pleased would they have felt that their construction was still serving its original purpose?

Of course, we don't know the definitive reason why people started building spires on the towers of their churches. A spire certainly points upwards to God, so that may be the reason; but it is equally likely to have been driven by engineering. Medieval engineers were inventive and ambitious, and when it became possible to build something unusual and complicated, they did so with gusto. Above all, though, a spire must have been a marker – a way of identifying a place both geographically and economically.

Back on the East Coast Main Line, think of the spires of Newark and Grantham. They are small towns today, and it's nice to know where they are, but why such extraordinary spires? These were towns on the Great North Road, the artery linking London and Edinburgh. These prosperous little places were vying with each other for the trade of travellers. Their spires reached higher than those in neighbouring towns like children in a classroom raising their hands higher in the hope the teacher would notice them first. These spires of England are the exclamation marks of our countryside. Punctuation that not only tells you where you are but helps you gauge the former economic condition and self-regard of a place.

Salisbury Cathedral now has the tallest spire in England (its great rival had been Old St Paul's in London, which lost its spire to a bolt of lightning during the reign of Queen Elizabeth I, and was then destroyed in the Great Fire of London of 1666). But what others lack in height, they make up for in number – Lichfield, for instance, with its three spires, is unique. But, for me, these competitions in spire envy are less interesting and beautiful than the village spires, seen half-shrouded in mist, set against a sunset or behind a flock of emigrating swallows, or glimpsed rising above a leafy tree canopy or against a filigree of bare branches and twigs. Rarely in the history of architecture have man and nature conspired to produce so much beauty.

SOUTH PARK, OXFORD

TIN MINES

Peter Watson

'As a photographer I am drawn to landmarks. On one occasion I was perched high above the Cornish coast, overlooking Wheal Coates tin mine. It was mid-February – cold, wet and inhospitable. And it was then I realised that Wheal Coates is much more than a landmark. This historic mine is an important part of Cornwall's heritage; it commands attention and is a striking reminder of another era. Long may its reign continue.'

MY CORNER SHOP

Daljit Nagra on local stores

Napoleon once mockingly described Britain as a nation of shopkeepers. And in many ways, when I consider the corner shops from my childhood, I think he was right. These shops were neatly ordered establishments. They pleased the eye as much as they displeased the pocket. They were convenience stores that were rarely convenient.

My parents often worked overtime at a factory, and if we ever fancied a dessert of tinned fruit cocktail with Carnation Evaporated Milk, the corner shop at the end of our road would certainly be shut. In fact, as I recall, it used to shut at 5pm on weekdays, with a half-day opening on Saturdays and was closed all day Sunday. There were frequent impromptu tea breaks (where a placard would be strung up saying: 'Back in a minute') and one-hour breaks for lunch.

The corner shop I revere is the Indian type that sprung up around the country from the late 1970s. They worked with the principle that shops should be emporia, and set about fulfilling this macro-ambition despite the shortage of space. As such, they cheerily ignored the logic that says things should be easy to find and to reach if you expect people to buy them.

In 1982, my parents bought a shop in Sheffield. The first thing we did was increase the opening hours to a simple numeric of 9am to 9pm, every day of the week – with no sneaky tea or lunch breaks. It had been a simple store that sold basic groceries, cigarettes and fresh bread from one bakery. But we soon had bread delivered from three bakeries to extend the choice; a video loan service; bouquets of flowers; daily copies of the Sheffield newspaper *The Star*; a fresh fruit and veg corner; a broken biscuit discount rack; stacks of 55lb sacks of potatoes; two deep freezers; a wide range of dairy produce in open shelved fridges and, best of all, we obtained an off licence and sold alcohol. We would have incorporated a postal service but, sadly, there was a post office in the area (which kept to the old British opening hours that left locals moaning in our shop…).

Our shop was like most Indian corner shops. We sold everything we could and packed it all in, on the simple principle of 'anything goes'. Sure enough anything did go, and while I rarely knew where things were (mops would sometimes be found alongside the video display and a stack of pink biscuits would peer from the crisps area), this approach seemed to encourage the customers to look harder so they would end up purchasing things they didn't even know they had wanted.

Despite the threat from supermarkets that seem to never, ever close, I am sure the corner shop will survive because people will always appreciate the local touch. After all, where else is a brief chat about the weather all part of the service?

CATHEDRALS OF SEWAGE

Maxwell Hutchinson on London's sewers

Down Abbey Lane in east London there sits a building that will never rank among the city's main attractions. Nobody notices its striking Byzantine-style elaborate flourishes or cruciform plan. Nobody misses its two Moorish-style chimneys from the skyline – they were demolished during World War II, condemned as a landmark for German bombers on raids over the city docks. But it is such a stunning building that its designers built two – its twin is situated at Crossness in south-east London. And because it's related to London's sewerage system, you'd hardly know it was there.

Even with this magnificent pumping station, otherwise known as a 'Cathedral of Sewage' or 'Mosque in the Swamp', the city's sewage system is all but invisible – a secret underworld beneath London's bustling streets. But when you think that every sanitary appliance in the metropolis is connected to these secret brick tunnels, it is, in fact, far more intriguing and engaging than a life above ground. If you could only see this underground maze – as I have been privileged enough to on several occasions – you would understand why it means so much to me. And why, in turn, it should mean so much to you. By removing the fear of waterborne disease it is helping keep us alive.

When the system was completed in 1875, London – along with most of the civilised world – had never seen anything like it. The city had grown exponentially following the Industrial Revolution and the health, social and economic problems this brought meant that diseases such as cholera were threatening the population. The first outbreak occurred in 1831. It was generally believed that the disease was airborne, carried in a mysterious vapour known as miasma. In fact, Florence Nightingale took this belief to her grave. The all-pervading fear of the miasma led the Victorians to drape their windows with heavy curtains in a vain attempt to keep the cholera at bay. The majority, however, drank the filthy water from the Thames, which was polluted with human sewage – most of the 369 sewers emptied into the river.

The problem was two-fold: the quality of drinking water and the means by which sewage from the growing metropolis could be safely removed. In 1849, Doctor John Snow, a physician from Soho who had carried out a survey of the health of those living within the catchment area of his practice, published the pamphlet *The Mode of Communication of Cholera*. He discovered that his patients who drank fresh well water from the pump in Broad Street, Soho, now Broadwick Street, avoided cholera. Those that drank from the local conduit, however, contracted the disease.

In parallel with Doctor Snow's work, Sir Joseph Bazalgette convinced parliament in 1858 to initiate the building of a gigantic network of underground sewers that would carry human effluent to the mouth of the Thames on the north and south banks. The effect of this massive endeavour on the health of Londoners was dramatic. Cholera epidemics were over for good.

The Bazalgette sewage system was emulated throughout the civilised world. It was pioneering in every respect and remains as effective today as it was 130 years ago. So when I look at the wonderful Abbey Mills Cathedral of Sewage, I don't mourn the loss of its chimneys. I remember the people who made this innovative idea possible – and beautiful in the process.

LIGHTHOUSES

Helen Dixon

'Lighthouses have been used to aid navigation for more than 2,000 years. Originally they were lit by wood fires or even the humble candle. Seafarers depend upon this beacon of light to protect them from the power of the sea and nature's elements. They add character to the coast and are a real achievement of modern engineering.'

ATTENTION
TO DETAIL

Sebastian Faulks, Leo Hickman,
David Lodge, Andy Goldsworthy,
Peter Ashley, Kurt Jackson

READING THE SIGNS

Sebastian Faulks on pub signs

The pub in the village where I was born was called The Three Horse Shoes. The sign hung in a timber frame at the top of a white post, the horseshoes making an inverted equilateral triangle, with the brewer's name, Ushers, in capitals underneath. To a child, everything about this sign was intriguing. We lived in horse country, between Newbury and Lambourn, and I was susceptible to the magic of the lucky shoe and number. The word 'Ushers' was also fascinating to me. I pictured men in long black gowns, going about some ancient brewing rite. Then there was the seedy romance of the pub itself. As well as a public and a saloon bar, The Shoes had an off-sales hatch, where an under-age errand-boy could be sent to fetch back bottles of Courage Light Ale. I couldn't wait to be old enough to go in, to breathe the forbidden air of beer and cool stone flags.

Between the ages of 20 and 40 I spent too much time in pubs. I loved the anonymity, the louche but friendly atmosphere. They were boozers then, which seldom had food, let alone a choice of Thai main courses. You went to drink ale and smoke. In the early 1970s, Watneys tried to do away with beer and substitute it with pressurised stuff that tasted of weak tea and soda water. I felt compelled to drink ever more real ale to keep the small brewers alive.

Any journey by car through England for me then was punctuated by the lucky dip of the pub stop. The signs themselves were often a good indicator. 'Fox and Hounds. Free House', with a jolly hunting scene was worth a look: proper beer and possibly some rudimentary food, such as sausage and mash. Anything with the word Watneys on the sign was out; not just out,

THE QUEEN'S HEAD

in fact, but to be sneered and hooted at. Courage pub signs became uniform, as I remember, and this was disappointing; it gave them a corporate feeling that was the opposite of what individual pubs with their quirky names should be. Courage was OK if nothing better was on offer. They had gone the fizzy route with their keg 'JC', but had retained proper bitter and a stronger, soupier brew called 'Director's'. Some people asked for lager. This puzzled me. It was like going to buy a shirt, being offered cotton or linen, but insisting on nylon.

The Marquess of Granby, The Wheatsheaf, The Queen's Head… these were usually reliable places. At Grantchester, near Cambridge, where I studied pubs with dedication, there was a Red Lion and a Green Man. One was everything a pub should be – open fire, real beer, dim lights; the other was bright, chilly and sold fizz. I can't remember which way round it was, but the last time I went to the village there was one called The Rupert Brooke. Oh well.

I expect there is a website somewhere which explains who the Marquess of Granby was and why so many pubs are named after him. Perhaps it also explains how the pub sign itself seems to follow only one design – as described above: the wooden playing card dangling in a frame or, in town, extended from brickwork on a wrought iron arm. I think this has an effect on the whole country. Whether you are walking in the Lake District or going home from work in Liverpool or Plymouth, you see this same rectangle, swinging free in wind or rain. The pub sign says: you are still in England. Come in here and – however far from home you are, however outlandish our name – you will find the comforts of your local town or village, the same drinks made by the same people, the same rows of

spirits behind the bar, the same salty crisps and, to be honest, much the same conversation.

Yet there is something daring and romantic about those names. I don't mean The Hippo and Peignoir, or deliberately silly ones. I mean The Jack of Diamonds or The Hare and Hounds. Perhaps those words, with their evocation of gaming and sports, lured too many good men to their doom. If they had been called the A641 Ring-Road Beer House would anyone have gone there? But who could resist the combination of the exotic and the familiar promised by such places as The Dundas Arms, Mother Black Cap, The Admiral Codrington, The Surprise, The Phoenix, The

Rowbarge and The Crooked Billet? They seem to reach down into a folk history that is rich and weird, to something pagan and ritualistic; yet they are as English as the downs from which you first see them swinging in the wind, like hanged men on a gibbet.

People who think of England as a practical country with little flair for the visual would never have imagined that its lanes and roads would be regularly punctuated by what look like cards from a wooden tarot pack – optical extravagances, creakily offering delight, escape and risk. But it is so; and sometimes we hardly see the strangest things by which we are surrounded.

CROSSING OVER

Leo Hickman on cattle grids

'D-d-d-d-d-d-d-d.' As a boy growing up in Cornwall, I loved the sound of cattle grids. Each time I saw one looming in the distance I would wince and grit my teeth in expectation of the fact our family car would always pass over it at several clicks faster than was probably recommended. Even now, it is the sound that comes to mind when I think about the countryside. I rank the percussive reverberations of rubber passing over metal bars at speed up there alongside the evocative call of the wood pigeon and the badger's bark.

And it seems I'm not alone. I smiled when I learned recently that the sound had been judged important enough to be recorded and placed into the British Library's archives as an official soundscape – 'a sound that is pertinent to a place' – of Dartmoor. It delights me to know that in decades to come students will stumble across the digital recording of cars passing over the cattle grid between Princetown and Two Bridges.

What I really love about the sound, however, is what it symbolises. It marks the border between a countryside that is tamed, neat and comforting, and one that is wild, tousled and close to danger. Cattle grids often tell us when we are entering common land – those fence-free stretches of common grazing that form some of England's most stunningly beautiful parcels of land. Cross a cattle grid and you can rest assured that, within a few minutes, a sublime moorland vista will present itself to you; a view of plaster-smooth undulations topped with granite, which have been maintained by countless generations of nibbling sheep, ponies, rabbits, deer and cows.

Cattle grids also represent ingenuity at its simplistic best. They perform that rare double act: an invention that offers perfect functionality – preventing the bother of stopping a vehicle and opening a gate – without tainting, hindering or damaging its surroundings. Animals are instinctively wary of them, to such an extent that on some highways in the US, black and white stripes are painted on road surfaces to trick animals into not crossing them. Children are also unnerved enough by their sight to approach them with caution. (I always feared that I would get my leg stuck as I tentatively crossed them by foot, and that the local farmer would then need to fetch a saw to perform an amateur amputation in order to free me.)

For me, however daunting a prospect, they will always be part of the landscape. But will evolution see their demise? It does seem some animals are trying cunning new ways to overcome these metal bars. In 2004, villagers in Marsden on the Yorkshire Moors reported seeing hungry sheep lying on their backs and rolling across cattle grids so they could reach fresh pasture. 'Sheep are quite intelligent creatures and have more brainpower than people are willing to give them credit for,' responded the National Sheep Association to the news. If only we could all live in fear of them forever – then this soundtrack to our countryside might never fade.

CATTLE GRID,
DARTMOOR

A TRADITIONAL
SIR GILES GILBERT
SCOTT PHONE BOX

WRITING STILES

David Lodge on stiles

There is no object more emblematic of rural England than the stile. Although I suppose other countries have them, they are especially characteristic of the English countryside, with its patchwork of fields bounded and protected by hedgerows and fences.

But, of course, a stile is more than a utilitarian device for passing from one field to another. There are no urban stiles, and to me, a child who first encountered country life in World War II as a displaced Londoner, stiles were novel and amusing structures, such as one might find in a playground. For adults, too, they have many uses: one may sit on them, stand on them, lean on them, use them for flirtation and courtship, conversation or confrontation. Symbolically they are liminal objects, marking a threshold – the passage from one state to another.

The classic English novelists were well aware of these possibilities. In *Jane Eyre*, for instance, the heroine first encounters Mr Rochester while sitting on a stile, where she has paused in the middle of a winter walk:

> *I sat down on a stile which led thence into a field. Gathering my mantle about me, and sheltering my hands in my muff, I did not feel the cold, though it froze keenly; as was attested by a sheet of ice covering the causeway…*

Along comes Mr Rochester on his horse, which slips on the ice, throwing its rider to the ground. Jane helps him up and, leaning on her, he hobbles over to the stile and sits down. In the conversation that follows, he identifies her as the governess who has come to look after his ward. She helps him remount, and goes on to complete her errand, musing on the incident:

> *It was an incident of no moment, no romance, no interest in a sense; yet it marked with change one single hour of a monotonous life.*

In fact, it has momentous consequences. It is Jane's unflustered helpfulness in their first encounter which leads Rochester to fall in love with her – by imprinting her on his consciousness as his rescuer in need, just as she will be at the end of the story.

In the Victorian age, when women were swathed in clothing from head to foot, the act of negotiating a stile – and thus showing an ankle or a flash of petticoat to accompanying males – was full of possibilities for coquetry and gallantry. There is a delightful example in *The Pickwick Papers*. Mr Pickwick and his companions, walking across the fields to Dingley Dell for the Christmas celebrations, meet Mr Wardle and his daughter, Emily, accompanied by a bevy of young ladies. Introductions take place without formality:

> *In two minutes thereafter, Mr Pickwick was joking with the young ladies who wouldn't come over the stile while he looked – or who, having pretty feet and unexceptionable ankles, preferred standing on the top rail for five minutes or so, declaring that they were too frightened to move. It is worthy of remark, too, that Mr Snodgrass offered Emily far more assistance than the absolute terrors of the stile (though it was full three feet high and had only a couple of stepping stones) would seem to require; while one black-eyed young lady in a very nice little pair of boots with fur round the top, was observed to scream very loudly, when Mr Winkle offered to help her over.*

The most striking use of a stile, however, must be in Hardy's *Tess of the D'Urbervilles*. When Tess, who has been seduced by Alec D'Urberville and is with child, is walking sadly back to her home village, she is overtaken by an artisan, carrying a pot of red paint. It is a Sunday morning. 'All the week I work for the glory of man,' he says, 'and on Sunday for the glory of God … I have a little to do here at this stile.' He stops, dips his brush in the paint pot, and…

…began painting large square letters on the middle board of the three composing the stile, placing a comma after each word, as if to give pause while that word

was driven well home to the reader's heart – 'Thy, Damnation, Slumbereth, Not'.

Against the peaceful landscape … these staring vermilion words shone forth… Some people might have cried 'Alas poor theology' at the hideous defacement … But the words entered Tess with accusatory horror. It was as if this man had known her recent history; yet he was a total stranger.

The English countryside had a better class of vandal in those days.

A STILE AT DEVIL'S DYKE, WEST SUSSEX

AN ARTIST'S IMPRESSION

Andy Goldsworthy on sheepfolds

A**s an artist, I am often asked about the objects and locations that have directly influenced my work. For me, inspiration lies not in grand structures or celebrated monuments. It lies in a sheepfold at Winton in the Eden Valley.

I first encountered this unimposing fold soon after moving to Brough in the early 1980s – most likely while on a walk up to the Nine Standards on Hartley Fell. It was early in my career and I had a part-time job working on the nearby Helbeck Estate, which involved doing minor repairs to dry stone walls. I was still some years from using folds and walls as part of my art. But when I think of the Winton sheepfold and the impression it made on me, it is fair to say this farming structure has played a huge part in my creative life. It certainly kindled my interest in folds as sculptural forms.

The Winton fold is just a simple, circular form. But what I still find so striking is the way the fold is sited. It sits in an open space – a collection point for sheep grazing out on the fell – and it provides an extraordinary focus for its surroundings. As you walk off the fells from open ground into fields that gradually become smaller and more defined, the fold begins to feel like an earthbound oculus.

In the late 1990s, as part of The Sheepfolds Project, I rebuilt and repaired 50 existing sheepfold, washfold and pinfold sites in Cumbria. Unfortunately, even though I was keen to work on the site of the Winton fold – with several proposals made to the village – I was refused permission to do so. It seems this uncomplicated agricultural mark on the landscape will always remain just beyond my reach.

TILBERTHWAITE GLEN STONE SHEEPFOLD IN CUMBRIA, REBUILT BY ANDY GOLDSWORTHY

FROM PILLAR TO POST

Peter Ashley on postboxes

The first pillar box I saw was at the end of our road. It had a cream oval on the top with the words 'Post Office' and a red arrow pointing to the shop door two yards away. My mother would lift me up in order to send letters skimming into the darkness, and I remember being there when the postman undid the door with a key from a huge jangling bunch and started shovelling the mail into a rust-coloured sack.

I knew from comics that burglars used sacks, and had to be dissuaded by my mother from the notion that a theft was being committed. I imagined that mail was collected in an underground cavern where tiny post elves – such as those in a Rupert Bear story – sorted it all out. The criminal element persisted when my brother told me that *when* (not *if*) I ended up in jail, all I could expect to be doing in my dungeon would be sewing mail bags.

Anthony Trollope is credited with introducing postboxes to the Channel Islands in 1852, long before knocking out his *Barchester Chronicles*. They arrived on the mainland a year later in Botchergate, Carlisle. It is odd that the experiment didn't start in the capital – usually the test bed for innovation. The first pillar box in our present monarch's reign was planted near the Horse Guards in 1952.

The royal connection took on new relevance when I bought the little I-Spy book *In The Street*, and postboxes became quarries in a hunting game to spot royal ciphers. These cast-iron monograms enabled a rough chronology to be applied; the flowing script for Victoria, the spare initials for George V. Even Edward VIII found his cipher cast on to a few boxes before he decided to throw in the crown. Much later I took pleasure in discovering the many variants of design. The early vertical-slitted box near Bishop's Caundle in Dorset; the acanthus leaves topping a Penfold hexagonal box in Chiswick; double boxes on city streets; airmail boxes in sky blue. And it's not just freestanding pillar boxes. Rural areas were served by boxes let into brick or stone walls; hump-backed and round-topped boxes clamped to tarred telegraph poles.

Icons of the English scene, pillar boxes stand like red and black guardsmen awaiting their orders. The perfect visual shorthand for communication, our digitalised cyberworld gives us nothing as potently recognisable. Remarkably, most of them are still with us, often all that stands between us and our messages, invitations, greetings and condolences reappearing – as if by magic – just about anywhere in the world. Occasionally they will be struck-off the postman's rota. But they still obstinately cling on to pavements, grass verges and walls. They are difficult to uproot; like icebergs there's almost as much below the pavement. One wall box – that once served Waddon Manor and other less grand abodes below Corton Down in Dorset – still revealed its fretwork grille sitting in the bottom when I cautiously opened the now unlocked heavy door. Apparently this is a snail trap, designed to prevent the shell-backed creatures from consuming the mail – how, I'm not quite sure.

I've always feared that these essential items in the iconography of England may one day disappear, or that in the spirit of the age I might wake up and find them all painted pale beige and owned by the Dutch. But I think there is now an agreement in place between the Royal Mail and English Heritage that conserves them. In the end though, it is down to us to care about them as much as we utilise them for their vital purpose.

A RURAL POSTBOX

THE WAY AHEAD

Kurt Jackson on milestones

At dusk, on the way to the pub for an early evening pint, I hesitate and linger at a familiar spot in the valley near my home. For at the junction that connects No Go By Hill, Nancherrow Hill and the Kenidjack Valley, there is a milestone. If you look closely, this triangular piece of granite suggests that Morvah is four miles and Botallack just one. But unless you know where to look, you'd hardly know it was there.

Marginalised and squeezed out by a widened and surfaced lane, and now repeatedly slapped by the road run-off, car splash and gritting machines, this milestone has seen better days. The back of the stone is against a wall with hanging ivy, valerian and robin song (above, a robin is seducing me with her evening chorus) that supports a contemporary chevron. Bold, black and white and unreservedly brash, it overshadows the older marker. The milestone seems almost invisible, especially now the curb stone has been built up to meet it. Its granite faces seem to resist almost anything – the odd chip betraying its age. But collecting litter and autumn leaves around its base, it looks as if it's lost its way.

There is something artistic about a milestone – but I am still unsure about its practical value. A coat of whitewash was once applied, and the pointing hands, letters and numbers that were carved into the surface have been filled with black pigment. It's all charmingly wonky, with almost childlike writing – wrapped around the stone as if the writer was running out of space. On other local examples where there wasn't enough room, the carver simply abbreviated the village names to become almost incomprehensible – other times they're misspelled or written out phonetically. I am not sure how many strangers would have stumbled across them at their prime and of what use they would be with incorrect names. And why would locals who know directions and distances need a hand? I do think, however, it's a style particular to our parish. You only have to go a few miles away and the lettering and design changes – capitals replace that immature font, the hand vanishes and the stones are shaped differently.

This simple stone is almost forgotten and definitely ignored by most passers-by; the leftovers from a time when travel was slow. The drivers are too fast and the pedestrians too familiar to pay any attention to its sharp edges or local detail. And even I must move on without its guidance. The robin has stopped singing, I'm getting cold, and I'm going to catch that pint. For the pub I'll take the unsigned way opposite, up Nancherrow Hill.

MILESTONE, CORNWALL

THE LIVING LANDSCAPE

Alice Temperley, Kate Adie,
Kevin Spacey, Tony Robinson,
Miles Kington, Charlotte Hollins

FORBIDDEN FRUITS

Alice Temperley on cider farms

BROWN'S APPLE,
SOMERSET

They are, for many, an integral part of our farming heritage. But our nation's cider farms and cider makers are not what they used to be. Growing up on a cider farm, we were taught from a young age to mourn the grubbing of an orchard. And I have done a lot of mourning since. In the past 50 years some 50% of Somerset's orchards have now disappeared. And the once familiar names of cider apples such as brown snout, chisel jersey and Kingston black sound ever more archaic.

It is perhaps because of their rapid demise that they are now, for me, rather melancholic places. But it wasn't always that way. The autumns of my childhood were dominated by the hum of the apple press and the smell of fermenting apples. On frosty mornings I would accompany my father to help fork pomace (crushed apple remnants) to the orchard's sheep.

Each autumnal apple harvest brought with it a wonderful sense of community. I will always remember the motley crew of apple pressers that would arrive before the first light around harvest time. At dawn – on especially cold days – I was in charge of taking this weather-worn team fried breakfasts. I always enjoyed their bawdy camaraderie, as they watched the sun rise over the mountains of apples piled in the yard.

In the orchard I was never alone. A notoriously fearsome pig called Ginger made a home among the apple trees. She – a bristling orange and black chicken-hunting monster – was a worthy pig to taunt. She was, however, a force to be reckoned with, and her infamous jaws were avoided only by mad dashes around nearby tree trunks. When the pig alone didn't provide enough excitement, we would brave her in plastic cider barrels – which we would clamber into before rolling down the orchard.

Of course, we would inevitably hit a tree, scramble out, and embark on the life-and-death tree-to-tree gauntlet before making it back to safe ground. Sadly, although the source of much enjoyment, Ginger the pig progressed from hunting and killing chickens to lambs and, after a stab at my mother's ankles, was banished to the freezer before she developed a taste for small children.

By preserving my memories, cider farms – with their vibrant apple trees – will remain the foundation from which I view the English countryside. They represent my childhood; I know and understand them. And, with any luck, they will continue to be an archetypal – albeit faded – vision of England in which I, too, can bring up my children.

IN SEARCH OF ENGLAND'S GNOMES

Kate Adie on deer parks

I used to wonder if deer were posh people's ornaments; the aristocratic equivalent of the garden gnome. For these animals do not seem real. They are never out of place in fairytales, myths and legends – the stories of Herne the Hunter and Robin Hood. And although our history books seem full of them – the royals grew forests to hunt them in, Georgian landowners created parks to show them off, and the poor used to enjoy feasting on them – not many people can claim to having ever seen one. But if you are lucky enough – as I was in my childhood – to catch these enigmatic beings on show, you'll soon realise the countryside isn't quite the same without them.

As a child, it was a treat to take a run in the car into Swaledale or Teesdale, away from the industrial cranes and pitheads of the County Durham coast. On the way back, full of egg and tomato sandwiches and homemade shortbread, we would always stop on the edge of the village of Staindrop. Once there, I'd peer over the dry stone wall towards the outline of Raby Castle and stare at its vast park of rather lumpy northern grassland, with a small copse here and there.

With luck came the moment when I could squeak: 'There they are!' as a clutch of brown thin-legged creatures would move tentatively into view – as if they'd been wondering whether it was worth putting themselves on show. Some would browse, others would stare snootily, and the antlered boss would stand at a distance, as king of the park. They always adopt a rather grand pose, which I found amusing when accompanied by their silly twitching tails.

Up close, deer are delightful, if a bit dim. They're not interested in being pets; they have no desire to please; they won't come when they're called and go bananas when a sheepdog appears. They seem made to decorate the countryside – when they feel like it – and they're rather good at it. Not only are they elegant, but they always come as something of a surprise. Unlike cattle and sheep, which can be relied upon to be more or less where you expect to find them, deer play Hide and Seek. On rural roads, there are signs saying 'Caution: Deer'. You proceed cautiously, expecting a stag to leap up to your bonnet, or plant itself foursquare and elk-like in the middle of the tarmac. But they somehow never appear. They are concealed in the greenery, waiting until you have passed, when they stroll out and probably congratulate each other on maintaining the view in the village pub that 'they may or may not exist.'

For many people, a deer will never be anything more than an image of Bambi in a picture book. But the chance to catch sight of the real thing is worth it. While elusive, they come into their own on country estates, when they eventually deign to graze in the sunshine. They stroll delicately, eyeing the landscape as they go – ready to bound into cover at the slightest hint of danger. Just watching them lets you imagine what it would be like to be a poacher in the Middle Ages, longing for a portion of tender meat to supplement a dull diet, or a newly-fortunate landowner dreaming of a landscaped park filled with handsome fallow and roe. For me as a child, the surprise of seeing deer was the icing on the cake, the unexpected bonus of a trip to the countryside. And waiting for them to appear was all part of the fun.

A RED DEER STAG DURING THE RUTTING SEASON

A SLOW BOAT TO BRISTOL

Kevin Spacey on canal boating

Having lived in London for a number of years, I've started to make a real effort to explore a little more of England's great countryside. The sheer volume of attractions, often peculiar-looking monuments and dramatic landscape makes any trip beyond the M25 sound pretty exhausting. But, I have to say, I'm never disappointed.

One of my favourite excursions last year was hiring a double-berth canal boat to cruise up and down the Kennet and Avon Canal – stopping off at every pub along the way. I know you English love to talk about the weather and it was amazing that weekend, with bright sunshine and little fluffy white clouds. It's a great way to watch the world drift by and it's a lot more relaxing – if a little faster perhaps – than travelling through London's streets. What better way is there to experience the spectacular Avoncliff Aquaduct and the nature that surrounds this man-made canal?

Of course, with every canal boating holiday comes the obligatory pub stop at one of the many drinking establishments that line the Kennet's banks. And it was at the Cross Guns pub, next to a beautiful old and deserted mill, with a stream running at the end of the garden, that I developed a taste for cider. In America, we don't drink much of the stuff – or at least I don't – so it was a lot of fun to discover that for the first time. It's also where I discovered how hard it is to steer a canal boat after three or four pints.

Cider wasn't the only highlight. Forget restaurant dining, eating on the roof of the boat under the stars – which are so much brighter than they are in London – is wonderful. And I would certainly recommend getting closer to – if not going in – the water. My friends had brought with them six inflatable dingys from Asda. One afternoon we ended up floating down the river that runs alongside the canal with our arms and legs hanging over the edge – very *Swallows and Amazons*. The river was freezing, but when the sun is shining and the water is so clear you can almost see the bottom, nothing else really matters.

Remarkably, I managed to survive the weekend without falling into the canal. But sadly the same can't be said for my little dog, Mini. She got elbowed off the boat and, rather amusingly, another friend – who was on the roof when it happened – dived in to save her. By the time he came up for air, however, she was on the bank of the canal shaking the water off her hair. We laughed a lot, but as you can imagine, he didn't.

I did get spotted as we were going through Bradford-on-Avon and found ourselves in a rather menacing-looking lock. There were lots of people around drinking in the pubs, and when one of the locals asked if I was Kevin Spacey, my friend thought it would be funny to tell him I was Kevin's double, Geoff. This became a running joke for the rest of the weekend.

The thing I love about the countryside is that you never quite know what you're going to get. The weekend after drifting through the wonderful West Country, I was up to my knees in mud at the Glastonbury Festival. But then, I suppose that's what makes it such fun. This year, I intend to make it to the Lake District for a slightly less muddy and eventful trip – although I hear it does rain a lot up there. I have been told such wonderful stories about it, and a friend suggested I might be able to hire Wordsworth's old cottage if I ask the right people. But perhaps I should leave the dingy at home this time!

ENGLAND'S COLOURFUL CANAL BOATS

YEOFORD

~72253

T SERVICES   NO

DIG FOR VICTORY

Tony Robinson on Mick Aston

Before I met Mick Aston, I thought archaeology was all about treasure hunting, and that an archaeologist's job involved digging enthusiastically into hillsides, and pulling out skulls and rusty swords. But under his tutelage, my eyes were opened to the fact that our archaeological heritage is an invaluable and irreplaceable part of our landscape – one that should be treated with love and respect.

One frosty morning early in our friendship he took me to the top of a church tower in the Welsh Marches. Below me was Much Wenlock, a typical little country town like so many others; the sort of place you'd stop off at to have a trawl round the gift shops, then drive on until you found a pretty country pub with an interesting lunch menu.

But Mick showed me a version of Much Wenlock that the casual tourist never sees. It was what he called 'the palimpsest of history' – the way the modern buildings overlaid the Georgian town, which cut through the Tudor plots that lie on top of the Norman street pattern, which itself surrounded a Saxon monastery. He pointed out how the tangle of streets and alleyways had a ruthless logic to them, how each one represented the needs of a particular group of people at a particular time in the settlement's history.

I could see why the town was built where it is, adjacent to a ford and at the head of a valley – the route between Wales and England for millennia. And beyond all this, I saw that what had initially seemed like a vague jumble of fields and hills were, in fact, medieval field systems, abandoned quarries and fish ponds, prehistoric burial grounds and Roman trackways.

The English landscape and its archaeology are under threat as never before from deep ploughing, inappropriate legislation, irresponsible metal detecting, theft, global warming and general ignorance. Mick Aston is a quirky, wise and Rabelaisian champion of our countryside who has inspired a generation of archaeologists (and armchair archaeologists) to look at our landscape as a portrait of change. It is a portrait we must cherish for the sake of future generations. I just wish there were more like him.

DOWN MEMORY LANE

Miles Kington on the family historian

Sometimes you can still see him, as dusk approaches, trudging along a country lane with the tools of his ancient trade dangling round him. He'll have his bags of notebooks, his laptop computer in its neat waterproof case, and condensed county guides and parish registers, sometimes reduced to the abstracted wisdom of a CD-Rom.

He is, of course, the family historian, driven by his quest for arcane knowledge and by the compulsion to explore his own family history. He is not always a welcome figure. Sometimes remote householders will peer out through their curtained windows and hastily draw the drapes shut as they see him come along the lane, pulling one of those trolleys used by fishermen, to transport all that genealogical knowledge. More often, clergymen with lone churches in their care, full of irreplaceable books of deaths, births and marriages, will spot him coming and shiver. They know that once the family historian is ensconced in a church, he may be there for days or weeks. Or even months.

Usually, there is just one family historian to each family. Nobody knows why, but each family seems to produce just the one member who acquires the urge to chart the furthest nooks and crannies of his own family tree. The rest of the family, if they ever had the incentive to follow the thin lines of descendants and forebears, are now quite happy to leave it to him.

It is always a 'him'. Very rarely does the family historian turn out to be a woman. Women are interested in people as people, not as strange names on a document. The gene that turns men into trainspotters, or into car experts, or into founts of knowledge about the personnel of jazz groups, must also be the same one responsible for transforming them into family historians.

And so he comes to build up the map of the family. The family historian is very good at asking the little questions (such as 'When Uncle Jack went off to make his fortune in Australia, is there any clue that he ever came back again?' and 'Who is this little bloke who keeps cropping up in family photos between 1920 and 1935 – his name is always crossed out so heavily that we don't know who he is?') but not so good at asking the big questions (such as 'What on earth am I asking all these stupid little questions for?').

I feel that being a family historian is an ancient craft, and that most of the old and grand families of England would have had their own archivist to keep the family tree in order. He might well have turned up as a character in a PG Wodehouse novel:

'I say,' said cousin Augustus, 'who's that queer cove wandering around in the library, wearing a moustache that wouldn't look out of place in the shellfish section of a fishmongers?'
'Oh,' said Aunt Mildred, 'that's young Wesley Snape. Your uncle has hired him to come and sort the family out.'
'Sort the family out? What's wrong with the family?'
'There's a whole lot of cousins missing in New Zealand in about 1890,' said Aunt Mildred.
'Good God,' said cousin Augustus. 'Mass murder, was it?'
'No,' said Aunt Mildred. 'Missing page in the family chronicle. Your uncle wants them all brought back and identified…'

But, of course, family historians do not turn up in modern novels. A novelist makes things up, and that would be anathema to a family historian. The noblest thing a family historian can do is go on dragging his family documents round with him, through the back lanes of old England, dragging back from obscurity characters that nobody ever knew existed in the first place.

HOW THE OTHER HALF LIVES

Charlotte Hollins on cattle

I often think it would be nice to live the simple life of a cow. I would spend the day munching various grasses and herbs from organic pastures and sitting down to chew the cud. Then, if I fancied a quick tipple, I would wander to the spring-fed pool, stroll into the woodland for a bit of shade from the hot summer sun before returning to graze the pastures again. It's all fairly tiring stuff!

My love of these domesticated ungulates stems from my earliest childhood memory. All I can remember is a vast landscape of grass, cows and, of course, the inevitable cow pats. I grew up on an organic farm in rural Shropshire and was inspired by my late father, Arthur Hollins, whose passion for the English landscape knew no bounds. Arthur was an eccentric man with a true love for Mother Nature and everything she created. He was continually surprised and excited by the miraculous way in which nature just takes care of itself. And, every time I wander through our fields, so am I.

With its varied habitats, unpredictable wildlife and stunning topography, England spoils us. I love the fact there is always so much life to look at wherever you are. I love the amazing way that each little bird, cow, small rabbit, each dung heap and tiny worm are all inextricably linked through the landscape; a landscape they have helped to create. I used to go for walks with my father and it wouldn't take long before he was down on his knees pulling apart a cow pat. He would talk for hours about the efficiency of worms in creating food for his pasture out of animal manure, and about the millions of other organisms that lived in that hidden and somewhat magical world beneath the surface of every landscape we see. For him, that was what made the landscape real and was why diversity in his grass pastures and a sustainable extensive grazing system for his cattle became so important. I love this world of hidden dimensions he created for me – and the fertility it provides. Without it, I wouldn't be able to watch my wandering cows and escape from the characterless urban scene.

It is not hard to see the attraction of lazy days in the pastures. But you would be wrong to think of it as a mindless activity. For it is the intelligence of these gentle giants that really fascinates me. When a calf is asleep in the grass, visited by surrounding butterflies, the mother will go and graze in another area of the field. If she feels that danger may be approaching – such as an unsuspecting human – she does not walk up to her calf, but will often walk in the opposite direction to attract attention away from her baby. It's a great trick – unless you are a farmer trying to bring the cattle in for checking and need to find the calf.

Without a doubt, my favourite time of year is late spring, when the calves are born. As they are out all year, our cattle graze on nothing but grass and we are used to seeing them in the fields. But when the cows move into the summer water meadows and the calves arrive, there is nowhere in the world I'd rather be.

HEREFORD CATTLE, DERBYSHIRE

SUPPORT OUR CAMPAIGN

Shaun Spiers, Chief Executive, Campaign to Protect Rural England (CPRE)

I hope the amazing variety of views and memories in this book, together with the stunning photographs, will inspire you to find out a little more about the Campaign to Protect Rural England. That we still have so much countryside and so many 'icons of England' left to celebrate is in large part down to the work of CPRE's volunteers and staff over many years.

But England is losing around 25 square miles of countryside every year, an area almost the size of Leicester. And half the country is disturbed by the sight or sound of development. Even in the countryside, it is getting harder and harder to 'get away from it all'.

So CPRE is much needed. We energetically and effectively oppose unnecessary developments, but we also make constructive proposals about how necessary development – not least, more affordable homes in rural areas – can be accommodated. And we support efforts to enhance the countryside, for instance by 'greening the Green Belt'. We want to protect the icons we have, but we also want to pass on to future generations even more that is worth treasuring.

Thank you for buying *Icons of England*. I hope you will now consider supporting our campaigns, joining us, volunteering with a CPRE branch, or making a donation. The English countryside, so wonderfully depicted in this book, really does need all the friends it can get!

CAN YOU HELP US?

By supporting the Campaign to Protect Rural England, you contribute to the continued existence of a beautiful, tranquil and diverse countryside for everyone to enjoy. You can help by:

• making a donation, regular gift or becoming a member of CPRE – and getting involved as much or as little as you want. Members receive our attractive magazine, *Countryside Voice* and discounted entry to over 200 beautiful, historic and stately houses and gardens across England. As a charity we rely on the generous support of people like you to help make our vision a reality;

• volunteering with your local CPRE branch, many of which organise events as well as campaigning at the local level. Volunteers are the grassroots of CPRE and are vital to our success;

• becoming a guardian of our countryside by leaving a legacy in your will.

Find out more about how you can help by visiting our website, www.cpre.org.uk, and the 'support us' section at www.cpre.org.uk/support. Or you can contact supporter services by emailing supporterservices@cpre.org.uk, telephoning 020 7981 2800 or writing to CPRE, 128 Southwark Street, London SE1 0SW.

EXMOOR, DEVON

CONTRIBUTORS

Kate Adie OBE became the BBC's chief news correspondent in 1989. She's won many accolades, including two Royal Television Society (RTS) awards and the Broadcasting Press Guild's Award for Outstanding Contribution to Broadcasting.

George Alagiah OBE presents *The BBC News at Six* and *World News Today*. He has won several awards including Amnesty International's Best TV Journalist. He is a patron of the Fairtrade Foundation and is an active supporter of Human Rights Watch.

Peter Ashley is a writer and photographer who champions everything that makes England such a unique and interesting place to live. He wrote *Unmitigated England* and *More from Unmitigated England*, and edited *Railway Rhymes*.

Clive Aslet is editor-at-large of *Country Life*. He writes for *The Daily Telegraph*, *The Sunday Telegraph* and *The Sunday Times*. His latest book *The English House* came out in autumn 2008.

Paul Atterbury is a writer, lecturer and broadcaster. His special interests include art, design and the history of canals and railways. He has written or edited over 30 books, and since 1990 has been one of the experts on the BBC's *Antiques Roadshow*.

Dr Muhammad Abdul Bari MBE, FRSA has worked as a researcher, teacher and SEN specialist in London. He is a trustee of the International Muslim Charity (Muslim Aid), and has been secretary general of the Muslim Council of Britain since June 2006.

Joan Bakewell is a broadcaster and writer. She began her TV career in the 1960s with BBC's *Late Night Line Up*. She now presents *Belief* on BBC Radio 3, and has a column in *The Independent*. She is chair of The National Campaign for the Arts.

Marc Bedingfield is a landscape photographer. His work is informed by the knowledge he gained whilst studying environmental conservation. www.marcbedingfield.co.uk

Richard Benson is a journalist who was brought up on a farm in Yorkshire. Helping his family with the enforced sale of the farm inspired his bestselling memoir, *The Farm: The Story of One Family and the English Countryside*. He is currently working on a non-fiction book to be published in 2009.

Raymond Blanc OBE is one of the finest chefs in the world. His Le Manoir aux Quat' Saisons has held two Michelin stars for over 22 years. He has written numerous bestsellers, including *Foolproof French Cookery*. He is now working on series two of BBC's *The Restaurant*.

Ronald Blythe is a writer and critic from Suffolk. Much of his writing reflects his East Anglian background. He is the author of *The Age of Illusion*, *The View in Winter* and *Akenfield: Portrait of an English Village*, which became an instant classic.

Rosie Boycott is a journalist and author. She has been editor of *The Independent*, *The Daily Express* and *Sunday Express* and is a regular guest on BBC

Radio 4's *Start the Week* and *Question Time*. Her latest book, *Spotted Pigs and Green Tomatoes*, was published in paperback in June 2008.

Derry Brabbs celebrates England's architectural and cultural legacy through his photographs. He has previously worked on books with Alfred Wainwright and has recently completed *Roads to Santiago*. www.derrybrabbs.com

Bill Bryson came to England in 1973 on a backpacking expedition and decided to settle. He wrote for *The Times* and *The Independent*, and has written many travel books, including *The Lost Continent* and *Notes from a Big Country*. He is also president of CPRE.

Sue Clifford lectured in natural resource planning through the 1970s and 1980s and was on the first board of Friends of the Earth. She helped found Common Ground and her work includes a book with Angela King, *England in Particular*.

Eric Clapton is a singer, songwriter and guitarist. He has had a successful solo career, as well as with The Yardbirds, Cream, and Derek and the Dominoes. He is the only triple inductee into the Rock and Roll Hall of Fame and has won or shared 18 Grammys.

Wendy Cope was a teacher for nearly 20 years and went freelance shortly after the publication of her first book of poems, *Making Cocoa for Kingsley Amis* in 1986. *Two Cures for Love,* a selection of poems from her books, was published in 2008.

Joe Cornish is one of Britain's most celebrated landscape photographers. He moved to North Yorkshire in 1993 to gain inspiration for his work, capturing the wild on film. www.joecornish.com

Nicholas Crane's books include *Clear Waters Rising: A Mountain Walk Across Europe* and *Mercator: The Man Who Mapped the Planet*. He is presenter of the recent BBC series *Coast*, *Map Man* and *Great British Journeys*.

General Sir Richard Dannatt was commissioned into the Green Howards in 1971. He has served seven tours of duty in Northern Ireland, with the UN in Cyprus, two tours in Bosnia, and in Kosovo. He became chief of the general staff in August 2006.

Helen Dixon specialises in the landscape and nature of South England. Rather than use digital photography, she uses filters to achieve her stunning images. www.helendixonphotography.co.uk

Guy Edwardes has been a nature and landscape photographer for 10 years. He draws much inspiration from the Dorset/Devon border where he lives. www.guyedwardes.com

Sebastian Faulks CBE is the author of 11 books, including *Human Traces*, *Charlotte Gray* and *Engleby*. He has been literary editor of *The Independent*, columnist for *The Guardian* and *The Evening Standard*, and is a fellow of the Royal Society of Literature.

Bryan Ferry is a singer and songwriter who came into prominence in the 1970s as the founder and lead vocalist of Roxy Music. He has since had a successful solo career, with eight UK top 10 solo albums.

Dick Francis CBE is an author and retired jockey. Following his first book, and autobiography, *The Sport of Queens*, he secured a 16-year position as racing correspondent at *The Sunday Express*. He has had a string of bestselling novels starting with *Dead Cert* in 1962.

Lee Frost lives in North Northumberland, strolling on its deserted beaches at dawn and dusk to inspire his breathtaking images. He is author of several acclaimed photography guides. www.leefrost.co.uk

Paul Gaythorpe is a freelance photographer, specialising in landscapes in North East England. His images have been featured in many magazines, books and calendars. www.pk4images.com

Andy Goldsworthy is an artist known for his outdoor sculptures and large-scale installations, such as 'The Sheepfolds Project' in Cumbria. His 2007 exhibition at the Yorkshire Sculpture Park was awarded the Southbank Award for Visual Arts.

Graham Harvey is agricultural story editor on *The Archers* and author of a number of books on food and the countryside. He wrote *The Killing of the Countryside*, which won the BP Natural World Book Prize. His latest book is *We Want Real Food*.

Tom Heap is a presenter. He is currently kept busy with *Costing the Earth* on Radio 4 alongside *Countryfile*, *Panorama* and *Animal 24:7* on TV. He worked at BBC news for 13 years, latterly as rural affairs correspondent.

Leo Hickman is a journalist and editor at *The Guardian*. He writes a column about ethical living and is the author of books including *A Life Stripped Bare: My Year Trying to Live Ethically* and *The Final Call: In Search of the True Cost of Our Holidays*.

Charlotte Hollins manages Fordhall Community Land Initiative at Fordhall Organic Farm. She saved the farm from developers in 2006 and it is now Britain's first community-owned farm.

Elizabeth Jane Howard CBE has written several novels, television plays and a collection of short stories. Her first novel *The Beautiful Visit* won the John Llewellyn Rhys Prize in 1951. Others include *The Long View* and *The Cazalet Chronicles*, which were televised on BBC1. Her new novel is *Love All* (published October 2008).

Chris Howe is a maths-teacher-turned-chartered-accountant and landscape photographer from Hertfordshire. www.chrishowephoto.co.uk

Margaret Howell was born in Surrey and has always loved the English countryside. A designer of contemporary clothes, she is inspired by natural fabrics and traditional British craftsmanship.

CONTRIBUTORS

Tristram Hunt is a lecturer in British history at Queen Mary, University of London and a fellow of the Royal Historical Society. He is author of *Building Jerusalem: The Rise and Fall of the Victorian City*.

Maxwell Hutchinson was president of the Royal Institute of British Architects from 1989 to 1991. He is a practising architect and contributor to BBC Radio 4 and BBC2's *Newsnight*. He presented Channel 4's *Demolition Detectives*, wrote and presented *No 57* and *The History of a House*, and worked on *First Sight* and *Restoration Nation*.

Kurt Jackson is one of Britain's leading painters. He embraces different materials and techniques. An understanding of natural history and ecology, politics and the environment is intrinsic to his art.

Simon Jenkins writes for *The Guardian* and *The Sunday Times*, as well as broadcasting for the BBC. His books include *England's Thousand Best Churches* and *England's Thousand Best Houses* and most recently, *Thatcher and Sons*.

Miles Kington was a writer for *Punch* who wrote humorous columns in *The Times* and *The Independent*. He was often on BBC radio and was the author of the popular series of books *Let's Parler Franglais!* He sadly died in January 2008.

Satish Kumar has been the editor of *Resurgence* for over 30 years. He is also director of programmes at Schumacher College. He has written many books including his autobiography, *No Destination*.

David Lodge is a novelist, critic and professor emeritus of English literature at the University of Birmingham. His new novel is *Deaf Sentence*. Other works include *Author, Author* and *Thinks*.

Richard Mabey is the author of some 30 books of literary non-fiction, including *Gilbert White: The Nature Man*, which won the Whitbread Biography Award. He is vice-president of the Open Spaces Society and patron of the John Clare Society.

Robert Macfarlane's first book *Mountains of the Mind* won the Guardian First Book Award and Somerset Maugham Award. His latest work *The Wild Places* won The Boardman-Tasker Award. He is a fellow of Emmanuel College, Cambridge.

Tom Mackie moved to Norfolk from the US in 1985. He has won many landscape photography accolades and is a regular contributor to *Photography Monthly*. www.tommackie.com

Andrew Marr is a writer and broadcaster.

Peter Marren writes about wildlife, the countryside and history. His books include *The New Naturalists* and *Twitching Through the Swamp*. He is currently working with Richard Mabey on *Bugs Britannica*.

Dr Richard Muir is the author of many books and articles on the history of the countryside, and has written a number of articles about landscape. He is an honorary research fellow in geography and environment at Aberdeen University.

Daljit Nagra is a poet. He currently lives and works in London as a secondary school English teacher. His first collection, *Look We Have Coming to Dover!* won the 2007 Forward Prize for Best First Collection and *The South Bank Show* Decibel Award in 2008.

Sean O'Brien is a poet, critic, playwright and professor of creative writing at Newcastle University. He received the Northern Rock Foundation Writer's Award in 2007. Much of his work has won awards, but most recently *The Drowned Book* was awarded both the Forward and TS Eliot Prizes.

Michael Palin CBE starred in the Monty Python sketches and films, as well as other TV series and films, including *A Fish Called Wanda*, which won him a BAFTA. He has also presented seven BBC travel documentary series.

Jonathon Porritt is a founder director of the sustainable development charity, Forum for the Future, chairman of the UK Sustainable Development Commission and author of *Capitalism as if the World Matters*.

Gavin Pretor-Pinney is founder of The Cloud Appreciation Society and co-founder of *The Idler* magazine. He wrote the international bestseller *The Cloudspotter's Guide*. His next book is about waves.

Lucy Pringle is a founder member of the Centre for Crop Circle Studies. She is regarded as an authority on the effects of electromagnetic fields on living systems. She is also an aerial photographer and has the UK's most comprehensive crop circle library.

Tony Robinson presents the Channel 4 series *Time Team*. As an actor he has appeared in several series, including *Blackadder*. He has written numerous books and won many awards from the RTS and BAFTA for his TV writing. He is president of the Young Archaeology Club.

Derry Robinson is a freelance photographer, concentrating almost exclusively on landscape. His work is regularly exhibited and published worldwide. www.derryrobinson.co.uk

John Sergeant is a broadcaster, journalist and writer, who has been Chief Political Correspondent at the BBC and Political Editor of ITN. He has written two bestsellers, one of which is his memoir, *Give Me Ten Seconds*.

Lucy Siegle is a journalist, author and presenter who specialises in ecological and ethical lifestyle matters. She contributes to *The Guardian* and *The Observer*, and magazines such as *Marie Claire*. She is the author of *Green Living in the Urban Jungle*.

Jon Snow has been with ITN since 1976 and has anchored *Channel 4 News* since 1989. He has won a BAFTA and been RTS Journalist of the Year twice, and he is a trustee of the Tate and National Gallery.

Kevin Spacey is an Academy Award-winning American film and stage actor and director. His role in *The Usual Suspects* won him his first Oscar in 1996 and, in 2000, he won the Best Actor for *American Beauty*. Since 2003 he has been artistic director of London's Old Vic theatre.

Sir Roy Strong is a prolific author. His latest book is *A Little History of the English Country Church*.

Alice Temperley launched Temperley London in 2000. It has quickly grown to become one of the most desirable fashion brands in the world. She has won awards from *Glamour* and *Elle*, the Walpole Award for British Design Excellence, and been named one of Britain's top 30 businesswomen.

Sir Nigel Thompson CBE, KCMG was chairman of CPRE from 2003 to 2008. He trained as a civil and structural engineer and spent his career at Ove Arup Partners, where he is currently non-executive deputy chairman.

Dr Simon Thurley is a leading architectural historian and chief executive of English Heritage. He has been director of the Museum of London, and curator of Historic Royal Palaces. He has written several books and is a regular broadcaster, presenting programmes such as *Houses of Power*.

Alan Titchmarsh is a gardener, author and broadcaster. He's written over 40 books and novels. Alan presented the BBC's *The Nature of Britain* and now has his own daytime ITV show, featuring conversation, music and the arts, and a Radio 2 music programme on Sunday evenings.

Sir Mark Tully was born in Calcutta and now splits his time between England and India. He was chief of the bureau for BBC New Delhi for 22 years and has written books such as *No Full Stops In India* and *The Heart of India*.

Charlie Waite is a landscape photographer who has published around 30 books and held exhibitions across Europe, the USA, Japan and Australia. His company, Light & Land, runs tours, courses and workshops worldwide. www.charliewaite.com

Chris Watson is a sound recordist who specialises in wildlife sounds from around the world. He has released solo CDs and worked across film, television and radio. He won a BAFTA award for Best Factual Recording on the BBC's *Life of Birds*.

Peter Watson's photographs capture the beauty of Britain's rural landscape. He is widely published and is the author of several practical photography books. www.peterwatson-photographer.com

Michael Wood is a historian and broadcaster. He is the writer and presenter of numerous acclaimed historical television documentary series including *Art of the Western World* and *Legacy*. Many of his recent documentaries are based on India.

Benjamin Zephaniah is a writer, poet and musician. He writes poetry that is musical and political, gaining much of his reputation through performance. He has published novels for teenagers as well as plays, and released numerous records.

PICTURE CREDITS

We would like to thank all of the photographers and photographic agencies that have generously supported CPRE and the publication of *Icons of England* by donating pictures for use in the book.

Marc Bedingfield: 62-63; **Derry Brabbs/CPRE**: 4, 15, 29, 64, 83, 101, 110, 115, 129, 142-143; **Britain on View**: 85; **Joe Cornish**: 24 (Britain on View), 25; **Helen Dixon**: 98, 140-141, 151, 162, 170; **Durham County Record Office: Durham County Library Collection D/CL 27/278 (uncatalogued)**: 94; **Guy Edwardes**: 14-15, 74-75; **Lee Frost**: 108-109; **Paul Gaythorpe**: 56-57, 71, 120-121; **Chris Howe**: 30-31, 40, 76; **Margaret Howell**: 58; **Rosamund Macfarlane**: 123; **Tom Mackie**: 114-115 (Alamy); 132-133; **MoD Directorate General Media and Communications**: 26; **Oxford Scientific Films**: 10, 17, 36, 39, 42-43, 51, 79, 80, 82-83, 100-101, 118, 161, 169; **Lucy Pringle**: 127; **Derry Robinson/CPRE**: 21, 69, 72, 88-89, 159; **Martin Trelawney/CPRE**: 86; **Charlie Waite**: 13, 68-69, 104-105; **Peter Watson**: 47, 136-137
All pictures from Alamy unless otherwise stated.

Headshots:

Bill Bryson: **David Rose**; George Alagiah: **BBC**; Richard Mabey: **Lizzy Orcutt**; Michael Palin: **Basil Pao**; Alan Titchmarsh: **Niall McDiarmid**; Clive Aslet: **David Banks**; Rosie Boycott: **Charles Glover**; Sean O'Brien: **Caroline Forbes**; Margaret Howell: **Jill Kennington**; Wendy Cope: **Caroline Forbes**; Eric Clapton: **Norman Watson**; Jon Snow: **ITN/Channel 4 News**; Michael Wood: **Joanna Vestey**; Peter Marren: **BBC Wildlife**; Ronald Blythe: **Nick Strugnell**; Daljit Nagra: **Sarah Lee**; Andy Goldsworthy: **Jonty Wilde**; Kate Adie: **Ken Lennox**; Miles Kington: **Geraint Lewis**

Captions:

14-15: High Cup Nick, North Pennines, Cumbria; limestone pavement, Malham, Yorkshire Dales (inset)
32-33: Burnham Beeches, Buckinghamshire; red admiral (inset)
50-51: Jetty on Lake Windermere; kingfisher (inset)
68-69: Spider's web in morning dew; frosted leaves, Leicestershire (inset)
82-83: St Michael's Mount, Cornwall; Great Tew, Oxfordshire (inset)
100-101: Rievaulx Abbey, Yorkshire; The Lady's Well, Holystone, Northumbria
114-115: Gunnerside, Yorkshire Dales in winter; ploughed field, North Yorkshire (inset)
128-129: Ancient thatched pub, Devon; dry stone wall, Yorkshire (inset)
142-143: Packhorse Bridge, Wasdale Head, Cumbria; footpath signpost (inset)
158-159: Gloucester Old Spot pigs on an organic farm, Exmoor; maize in Hampshire (inset)